SUMMER BRAIN QUEST

Dear Parent,

At Brain Quest, we believe learning should be an adventure—a *quest* for knowledge. Our mission has always been to guide children on that quest, to keep them excited, motivated, and curious, and to give them the confidence they need to do well in school. Now, we're extending the quest to summer vacation! Meet SUMMER BRAIN QUEST: It's a workbook. It's a game. It's an outdoor adventure. And it's going to stop summer slide!

Research shows that if kids take a break from learning all summer, they can lose up to three months' worth of knowledge from the previous grade. So we set out to create a one-of-a-kind workbook experience that delivers personalized learning for every kind of kid. Personalized learning is an educational method where exercises are tailored to each child's strengths, needs, and interests. Our goal was to empower kids to have a voice in what and how they learned during the summer, while ensuring they get enough practice with the fundamentals. The result: SUMMER BRAIN QUEST—a complete interactive program that is easy to use and designed to engage each unique kid all summer long.

So how does it work? Each SUMMER BRAIN QUEST WORKBOOK includes a pullout tri-fold map that functions as a game board, progress chart, and personalized learning system. Our map shows different routes that correspond to over 100 pages of curriculum-based exercises and 8 outdoor learning experiences. The variety of routes enables kids to choose different topics and activities while guaranteeing practice in weaker skills. We've also included over 150 stickers to mark progress, incentivize challenging exercises, and celebrate accomplishments. As kids complete activities and earn stickers, they can put them wherever they like on the map, so each child's map is truly unique—just like your kid. To top it all off, we included a Summer Brainiac Award to mark your child's successful completion of his or her quest. SUMMER BRAIN QUEST guides kids so they feel supported, and it offers positive feedback and builds confidence by showing kids how far they've come and just how much they've learned.

Each SUMMER BRAIN QUEST WORKBOOK has been created in consultation with an award-winning teacher specializing in that grade. We cover the core competencies of reading, writing, and math, as well as the essentials of social studies and science. We ensure that our exercises are aligned to Common Core State Standards, Next Generation Science Standards, and state social studies standards.

Loved by kids and adored by teachers, Brain Quest is America's #1 educational bestseller and has been an important bridge to the classroom for millions of children. SUMMER BRAIN QUEST is an effective new tool for parents, homeschoolers, tutors, and teachers alike to stop summer slide. By providing fun, personalized, and meaningful educational materials, our mission is to help ALL kids keep their skills ALL summer long. Most of all, we want kids to know:

It's your summer. It's your workbook. It's your learning adventure.

—The editors of Brain Quest

This book belongs to:

_____

Library of Congress Cataloging-in-Publication Data is available.

ISBN 978-0-7611-8920-6

Summer Series Concept by Nathalie Le Du, Daniel Nayeri, Tim Hall
Writers Bridget Heos, Claire Piddock
Consulting Editor Kim Tredick
Art Director Colleen AF Venable
Cover, Map, Sticker, and Additional Character Illustrator Edison Yan
Illustrator Chad Thomas
Series Designer Tim Hall
Designers Abby Dening, Carolyn Bahar, Tae Won Yu
Editor Nathalie Le Du
Production Editor Jessica Rozler
Contributing Editor Kim Tredick
Production Manager Julie Primavera

Workman books are available at special discounts when purchased in bulk for premiums and sales promotions as well as for fund-raising or educational use. Special editions or book excerpts can also be created to specification. For details, contact the Special Sales Director at the address below, or send an email to specialmarkets@workman.com.

DISCLAIMER
The publisher and authors disclaim responsibility for any loss, injury, or damages caused as a result of any of the instructions described in this book.

Workman Publishing Co., Inc.
225 Varick Street
New York, NY 10014-4381
workman.com

BRAIN QUEST, IT'S FUN TO BE SMART!, and WORKMAN are registered trademarks of Workman Publishing Co., Inc.

Printed in China
First printing March 2017

10 9 8 7 6 5 4 3 2 1

BETWEEN GRADES 4 & 5

For adventurers ages 9–10

Written by Bridget Heos and Claire Piddock
Consulting Editor: Kim Tredick

WORKMAN PUBLISHING

NEW YORK

Contents

Instructions 5

Level 1 9

Level 2 16

Level 3A 22

Level 3B 34

Level 4A 48

Level 4B 58

Level 5A 68

Level 5B 82

Level 6A 96

Level 6B 112

Summer Brainiac Award! 128

Outside Quests 129

Answer Key 134

Summer Brain Quest Reading List 145

Summer Brain Quest Mini Deck 154

4

SUMMER BRAIN QUEST®

Your Quest

Your quest is to sticker as many paths on the map as possible and reach the final destination by the end of summer to become an official Summer Brainiac.

Basic Components

Summer progress map

100+ pages of quest exercises

100+ quest stickers

8 Outside Quests

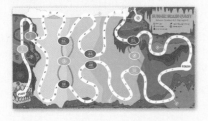

8 Outside Quest stickers

Over 30 achievement stickers

Summer Brainiac Award

100% sticker

Setup

Detach the map and place it on a flat surface.

Begin at **START** on your map.

How to Play

To advance along a path, you must complete a quest exercise with the matching color and symbol. For example:

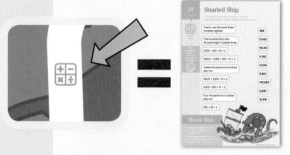

Math exercise from the orange level (Level 2)

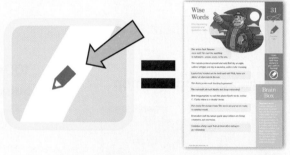

English language arts exercise from the red level (Level 3A)

Social studies exercise from the blue level (Level 5A)

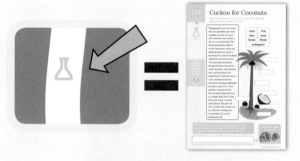

Science exercise from the green level (Level 6B)

If you complete the challenge, you earn a matching quest sticker.

Place the quest sticker on the path to continue on your journey.

 At the end of each leg of your journey, you earn an achievement sticker.

Apply it to the map and move on to the next level!

Forks in Your Path

When you reach a fork in your path, you can choose which direction to take. However, each level must be completed in its entirety. For example, you cannot lay two quest stickers down on Level 3A and then switch to Level 3B.

If you complete one leg of the level, you can return to the fork in the path and complete the other leg.

Outside Quests

Throughout the map, you will encounter paths that lead to Outside Quests.

To advance along those paths, you must complete one of the Outside Quests.

If you complete an Outside Quest, you earn an Outside Quest sticker and advance toward 100% completion!

Bonuses

If you complete a bonus question, you earn an achievement sticker.

BONUS: Write a sentence about a platypus's day, using a progressive verb.

_____

_____

_____

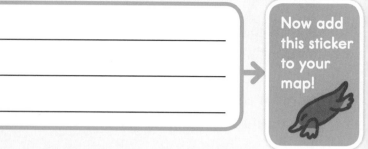

Now add this sticker to your map!

Subject Completion

If you complete all of the quest exercises in a subject (math, English language arts, science, or social studies), you earn an achievement sticker.

CONGRATULATIONS! You completed all of your English language art quests! You earned:

Summer Brainiac Award

Presented to:

_____

for successfully completing the learning journey in
SUMMER BRAIN QUEST®: BETWEEN GRADES 4&5

Summer Brain Quest Completion Sticker and Award

If you complete your quest, you earn a Summer Brain Quest completion sticker and award!

QUEST complete!
Welcome to 5th grade!

100% Sticker

Sticker _every_ possible route and finish _all_ the outside quests to earn the 100% sticker!

Level 1

Hot Diggity!

Complete the crossword puzzle by filling in the blanks with a relative adverb or relative pronoun from the box. (HINT: You can use each word more than once.)

Relative Adverbs and Pronouns

Upon completion, add this sticker to your path on the map!

where
when
why
that
which
who
whom
whose

Across

2 The parts of bone ____ were alive decayed over time.

3 Colorado is ____ dinosaurs once roamed.

4 Their bones, ____ were buried over time, can still be found here.

5 I told my friend Leo, ____ is a dinosaur nut, first.

6 Last summer was ____ I found the bone.

Down

1 Over time, the land eroded and the dinosaur bones, ____ had become rocks called fossils, were found.

3 Dinosaur Ridge is ____ I spotted the bone.

4 The company ____ backhoe we rented was called Dinodiggers.

5 The reason ____ I didn't tell anyone at first was that I wanted to study it myself for a while.

6 Dr. Pretzel, ____ Leo knows from Archeology Camp, also came to see the fossil.

Here Be Pirates!

Read the document. Then answer the questions.

Primary Documents

Upon completion, add this sticker to your path on the map!

I. Every man shall have equal say as to who shall be captain.

II. Every man may eat and drink at his pleasure, unless hunger should strike this ship.

III. After a plundering attack, all men shall be given equal shares, excepting the captain, doctor, and carpenter, who shall be given double.

IV. Every man shall keep his pistol and cutlass clean and fit for engagement or else shall lose his share of the loot.

V. If a man loses an eye during battle, he shall have 50 gold pieces; half a limb, 100 pieces; a whole limb, 200 pieces. He shall be allowed to stay aboard as long as he sees fit.

VI. Any man caught stealing from man or ship shall be marooned on a desert island.

VII. Any man who deserts ship during battle shall suffer certain death.

Brain Box

A **primary source** is a direct account, document, or object created during the time period being studied, for example, a letter written by a Civil War soldier, or a video interview with a witness to an event.

For whom was this document written? _____

Who likely wrote the document? _____

What is the purpose of this document? _____

_____

Choose one of the rules and write it in your own words.

_____

_____

Which rule do you think is most important and why?

_____

_____

You found the following items in a buried tunnel. Underline the primary sources.

Stone Age tool

cave art

an article about Neanderthals

an explorer's diary

Now add this sticker to your map!

Rocks and
Minerals

Rock Star

Read about each rock or mineral's history.
Then label each mineral, sedimentary rock,
igneous rock, or metamorphic rock.

You might say I had a rather explosive start.
I was shot out of a volcano and fell to the
ground as a lightweight rock called pumice.
I'm holey because of the air trapped as the
lava cooled. These holes are what make me
so lightweight that I can even float on water!

_____

The two words that best describe me? Solid
gold. In fact, I'm made up of a single element.
I existed as shiny flakes on other rocks,
but was eroded by wind and water. Because
I was so heavy, I sank to the bottom of a
stream. Then people scooped me up and
melted me into a big old block of gold.

_____

Upon
completion,
add this
sticker to
your path on
the map!

I got off to a rather rocky start. I used to be a type
of sedimentary rock called limestone. But then I was
pushed underground, where things got hot. Not lava
hot. But still hot. Now, I'm one of the most beautiful
rocks in the world: marble. How marble-lous!

_____

Brain Box

A **mineral** is a substance whose properties are the same throughout.

A **rock** is composed of one or more minerals. There are three types of rocks:

• A **sedimentary rock** forms when ice, water, and wind erode land and deposit the
sediment somewhere else. The sediment builds up and is compacted into rock.

• An **igneous rock** forms when magma or lava cools and solidifies.

• A **metamorphic rock** forms when either an igneous or sedimentary rock
changes because of heat or pressure.

Jumping Jerboa

Compare the value of the numbers using place value. Fill in the multiplication and division equations.

Hundred Thousands	Ten Thousands	Thousands	Hundreds	Tens	Ones

$20,000 \div 20 = \underline{1,000}$

$20,000 = 20 \times \underline{1,000}$

Hundred Thousands	Ten Thousands	Thousands	Hundreds	Tens	Ones

$7,000 \div 700 = \underline{\qquad}$

$7,000 = 700 \times \underline{\qquad}$

Hundred Thousands	Ten Thousands	Thousands	Hundreds	Tens	Ones

$5,000 \div 50 = \underline{\qquad}$

$5,000 = 50 \times \underline{\qquad}$

Hundred Thousands	Ten Thousands	Thousands	Hundreds	Tens	Ones

$30,000 \div 30 = \underline{\qquad}$

$30,000 = 30 \times \underline{\qquad}$

So Much Energy!

Write whether the energy is being transferred through a collision, sound, light, heat, chemical reaction, or electric currents.

Transfer of Energy

Upon completion, add this sticker to your path on the map!

_____

_____

_____

_____

_____

_____

Brain Box

Energy cannot be created or destroyed. However, it can be transferred from one thing to another through a **collision, sound, light, heat, chemical reaction,** or **electric currents.**

BONUS: The chemical compounds in a stingray's stomach break down food and release energy, which allows the stingray to swim some more. What kind of energy is the food? Circle one.

chemical

electric

sound

light

Now add this sticker to your map!

Level 1 complete!

Add this achievement sticker
to your path...

...and move on to

Level 2!

You're the Archeologist

Read the descriptions of Native American peoples. Then draw a line from the artifacts and landmarks to the correct regional peoples.

Pacific Northwest

Peoples of the Pacific Northwest, including the Makah and Chinook, enjoyed food from both land and sea. Food was so plentiful that not everyone needed to hunt and gather. Some focused on art instead, creating elaborate totem poles.

Southwest

In deserts in the Southwest, tribes such as the Hopi, Navajo, and Apache used irrigation to grow beans, corn, and squash. With few available trees with which to build homes, they used a mixture of mud and straw called adobe. Droughts were devastating to Southwest peoples and often led to war and famine.

Brain Box

Artifacts and **landmarks** can help an archeologist understand a group of people that lived in the past.

Midwest and Southeast

People of the Mississippian culture, who were likely ancestors of tribes such as the Cherokee, Kansa, and Missouria, farmed corn. This plentiful crop gave rise to cities such as Cahokia, where more than 20,000 people once lived. Most citizens worked the fields, but others constructed the city's 100-foot-tall mounds, upon which the city's ruling class lived and worked.

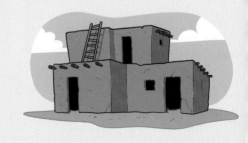

Worst Picnic Ever

Underline the progressive verbs.

Progressive Verbs

Upon completion, add this sticker to your path on the map!

Today I packed a picnic and headed to the beach—barefoot as always. While I <u>was walking</u>, I noticed an eerie stillness. But I brushed it off because, aside from the clouds in the distance, it was a bright, sunny day. So sunny, in fact, that I should have worn flip-flops! I was running to the water to cool my feet when my picnic spilled out of the basket. I grabbed the cookies first, and as I did, a seagull swooped in. I tried to chase it away, but it already was tearing open the sandwich bag. Ugh. Now it was a covered-in-sand-wich. By now, my feet were on fire! I ran to the water, where I promptly dropped the cookies. As I reached for them underwater, I realized I was soaking the chips, too. And that's when I looked up and came face-to-face with a shark. Now it was eyeing ME for a picnic lunch. I dropped everything and swam back to shore. I started over to warn the lifeguard, but realized she was clearing the water already. The clouds had rolled in, and a massive water spout was forming out at sea. It was heading our way! Everyone was running to their cars, and someone plowed right into me. I fell to the ground, thinking, "If I don't hurry, I will be flying through the air in a water spout!" I got myself up and raced home. Now I am sitting in the kitchen, soaked, spooked, and starving. If anyone asks how my day went, I will be telling them that it was no picnic!

BONUS: Write a sentence about a platypus's day, using a progressive verb.

_____

_____

_____

Now add this sticker to your map!

Snarled Ship

Draw lines to match the numbers in words or expanded notation with the number in standard form.

Number Names

Upon completion, add this sticker to your path on the map!

Twenty-one thousand three hundred eighteen	**386**
One hundred forty-five thousand eight hundred three	**12,162**
2,000 + 600 + 20 + 6	**45,813**
40,000 + 5,000 + 800 + 10 + 3	**4,262**
Twelve thousand one hundred sixty-two	**12,016**
10,000 + 2,000 + 10 + 6	**5,813**
5,000 + 800 + 10 + 3	**145,803**
Four thousand two hundred sixty-two	**2,626**
300 + 80 + 6	**21,318**

Brain Box

The **standard notation** for a number is the way it is typically written.
Example: 5,312

The **expanded notation** shows the place value of each digit in the number.
Example: 5,000 + 300 + 10 + 2

Secret Code

The lighthouse reveals a secret code to open the pirate's treasure chest. Follow the instructions to discover the code.

Write the expanded notation for each number.

Comparing Multi-Digit Numbers

	Thousands		Hundreds		Tens		Ones
2,287 =		+		+		+	
5,256 =		+		+		+	
8,543 =		+		+		+	
6,911 =		+		+		+	
7,943 =		+		+		+	
7,921 =		+		+		+	

Write the numbers in order from least to greatest.

_____ < _____ < _____ < _____ < _____ < _____

Circle the digits in the ones place. Then write them in the order they appear above to form the code.

____ ____ ____ ____ ____ ____

BONUS: Write the code in expanded form.

Now add this sticker to your map!

A Shiny Red Surfboard

Study the chart. Then write each set of adjectives in the correct order.

Number	Descriptive	Size	Age	Shape	Color	Origin	Material	+ Noun
two	fast	little			silver			fish
a	quaint		old			New England		lighthouse
the				circular	black		wooden	table

surfboard
red
lightweight
a

a lightweight red surfboard

beach
crowded
the
city

_____

mermaids
brave
young
two

_____

shark
dangerous
white
a

_____

island
uninhabited
an
Pacific

_____

Brain Box

When multiple **adjectives** are used in a sentence, they should be placed in a certain order, as shown above.

Level 2 complete!

Add this achievement sticker to your path…

…and move on to
Level 3A
on page 22!

…or
move on to
Level 3B
on page 34!

Mythology

START
LEVEL
3A
HERE!

The Wall

Read the myth.

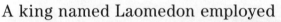

Long ago, Poseidon, the Greek god of the sea, rose up against his brother Zeus, the god of earth and sky. Poseidon's co-conspirator was Zeus's own son, Apollo. Just as Zeus prepared to hurl the traitors into the underworld, Apollo's mother, Leto, intervened. Zeus agreed not to kill the traitors but demanded that they do penance instead. For one year, they would work as servants to a mortal man.

A king named Laomedon employed Poseidon and Apollo to build a wall of protection around the city of Troy. If they finished the job in one year, they would be paid fairly. However, it was all a trick; the king knew it was impossible for two men to build the wall in a year's time. Of course, these weren't men but gods, and so day by day, night by night they laid stones, finishing the job on the last day. Now a wall fully encircled Troy, save for the entrance. Seeing this, the king deemed the wall incomplete and refused to pay. Thus Apollo hired a mortal to complete the wall so that it would be weak in that section.

However, Poseidon craved more immediate justice. He made the sea rise up until it reached the city walls. With its farmland flooded, Troy was in trouble. The waters would only recede when a sea monster dwelling in its waves was appeased. The people of Troy made animal offerings to the monster, but it demanded more: a human sacrifice. The people of Troy drew straws to see who would be eaten. To everyone's surprise, Laomedon's own daughter, Hesione, drew the smallest straw.

As luck would have it, the hero Heracles happened by that day for a visit. He offered to slay the monster for a small price: two of Laomedon's finest horses. The king agreed, and so Heracles swam out to the monster and slayed it with a bow and arrow. The waters receded and the people rejoiced. But the cheap king reneged on his offer of the horses. Heracles raised an army against Troy, which entered at the weak spot in the wall and defeated the city.

Complete a comic strip version of the story. Include narration and speech bubbles for the characters. Then answer the question.

Upon completion, add this sticker to your path on the map!

How are gods like Zeus and Poseidon similar to superheroes?

_____

_____

_____

_____

_____

European Explorers

Map Mishap

Study each map and read the captions. Then answer the questions.

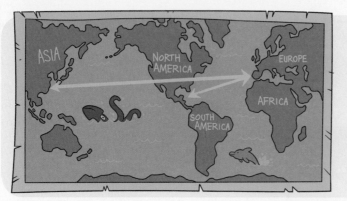

Modern Map

This modern map shows the actual distance from Europe to Asia and the distance of Columbus's voyage to America.

Ptolemy's Map

In 125 CE, Claudius Ptolemy knew the correct circumference of the earth but he thought that Asia was larger than its actual size. Therefore, he thought the Asian continent was the equivalent of 11,000 kilometers away. And because he did not know that the Americas existed, they aren't on his map.

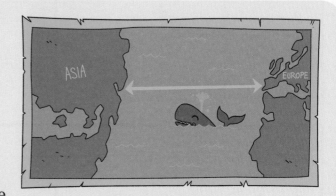

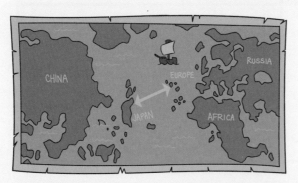

Columbus's Map

Columbus relied on Ptolemy's map to find a new route to Asia. But he made a mistake. Ptolemy gave the circumference of the earth in Arabic units. Columbus thought these were the same as Roman miles, but Roman miles were actually much shorter.

Which map was closer to being correct about the distance from Europe to Asia—Columbus's or Ptolemy's? _____

What continents are both Columbus's and Ptolemy's maps missing?

_____

Why does Columbus's map show a shorter distance between Europe and Asia than Ptolemy's?

_____

_____

Comma Drama

Fill in the missing commas. (HINT: You need to add 14 commas in all.)

Where are we Diya?

I don't know Ryan. But we're alive and that's the important thing. Now we need to find fresh water food and large stones.

What are the large stones for Diya?

Well we need to make an S.O.S. sign. If rescuers fly over us they'll see it.

Okay but let's find something to eat first because I'm starving.

Do you realize we're going to have to fish hunt or scavenge for our food?

Why can't we just order something from that tiki hut?

Oh I guess this isn't a deserted island after all.

Upon completion, add this sticker to your path on the map!

Fish School

Look at the fish. Use each measurement to find the products.

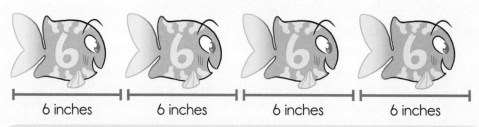

6 inches   6 inches   6 inches   6 inches

A new fish comes to school that is 4 times as long as the green fish. How long is the new fish?

$$4 \times \underline{\quad} = \underline{\quad} \text{ inches}$$

How many times longer is the blue eel than the green fish?

$$18 = \underline{\quad} \times 6$$

☐ times longer

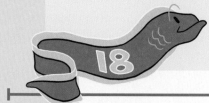

18 inches

If 6 fish fit in this school, how many fish would be in a school that is 5 times as big?

$$6 \times \underline{\quad} = \underline{\quad} \text{ fish}$$

How many times longer is the red fish than the green fish?

$$6 \times \underline{\quad} = 12$$

☐ times longer

12 inches

Fishing for Answers

Draw a line to match each word problem with the correct equation. Then solve each word problem.

Multiplication and Division Comparisons

Flying fish can jump up to 6 meters. How many times higher is that than a person who can jump 2 meters?

_____

$13 × 3 = e$

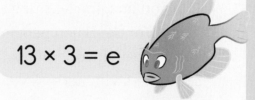

An adult whale shark has 4,000 teeth. A baby whale shark has 10 teeth. How many times more teeth does an adult have than a baby?

_____

$6 ÷ 2 = j$

$10 × t = 4,000$

Upon completion, add these stickers to your path on the map!

If a red snapper weighs 40 pounds, how many times heavier is a red snapper than a fish that weighs 8 pounds?

_____

$6 × 2 = y$

$s = 40 × 8$

A human eye can be 3 centimeters long. An octopus has an eye 13 times as long. How long is the octopus eye?

_____

$40 ÷ 8 = r$

BONUS: Hammerhead sharks can live in schools of 500 sharks. How many times larger is a hammerhead school than a school of 50 angelfish?

Now add this sticker to your map!

The Bajau

Read the story. Then answer the questions.

Born to Swim: Life on the Water

Can you imagine learning to swim before you even learned to walk? For the Bajau people of Southeast Asia, that's a way of life. They live and work on boats or in sea homes. As a result, they are great swimmers—even from a young age.

Traditionally, the Bajau have lived in houseboats. Those who still do are so used to life at sea that on land they can feel land sick. Recently, some Bajau have settled in houses on stilts that rise out of the sea. These houses are often connected by wooden boardwalks so that people can walk from house to house. When there is no such boardwalk, people swim to other houses to visit their friends and family.

The Bajau make a living by fishing. They eat the fish and shellfish they catch, and they also trade them for rice and drinking water. The men have a unique way of fishing. They dive up to 66 feet (20 meters) deep. Then they walk along the bottom of the ocean, spearing fish, octopus, squid, and sea cucumbers while holding their breath for up to 5 minutes at a time. Meanwhile, the women gather sea urchins, sea cucumbers, and clams along the shore, and take a boat to a nearby market to sell them.

Children help their families fish, learning the skills as they grow. However, life at sea isn't all work, work, work. Bajau children have time to play, jumping from the walkways into the water and diving deep just for fun.

Circle the main idea of the text.

Bajau children like to have fun.

Bajau people live, work, and play on the ocean.

Fish provide a healthy diet to the Bajau people.

Underline the key details in the text that support the main idea.

For Bajau people who live in houseboats, what often happens to them on land?

_____

How does fishing differ for Bajau men and women?

_____

_____

Write three sentences stating why you would or would not want to live like the Bajau people. Use key details from the text to support your answer.

_____

_____

_____

BONUS: Historically, gulls that fed along seashores hunted small marine animals. Now, gulls also scavenge for food scraps and have moved inland to forage in dumpsters and landfills. How have the birds' eating habits adapted to the activity of people?

_____

_____

_____

_____

Now add this sticker to your map!

Upon
completion,
add this
sticker to
your path on
the map!

Across the Pacific

Draw a dot on the map for each given location, based on the coordinates. Then connect the dots to chart your course.

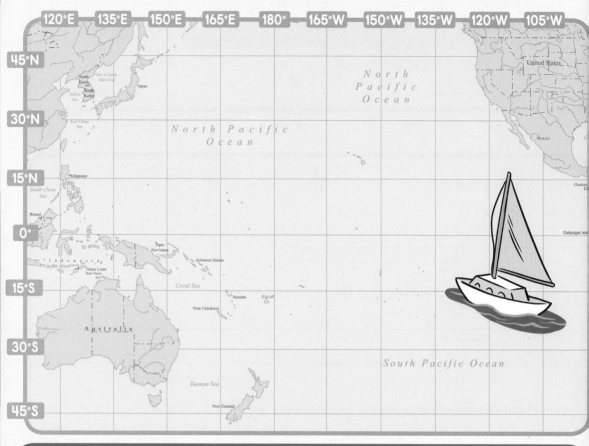

Brain Box

Latitude is the measurement of degrees between the **equator** and any line parallel to it. **Longitude** is the measurement of degrees between the **Greenwich meridian** and any line that intersects it at the North and South Poles.

 Set sail from Santa Barbara, California, 35 degrees N, 120 degrees W.

 Visit Mauna Loa, an active volcano and scientific observatory, on Hilo Island, Hawaii, 20 degrees N, 155 degrees W.

 Next, travel to Caroline Island, 10 degrees S, 150 degrees W, to study the seabirds and coconut crabs.

 Go to Samarai Island in Papua New Guinea, 10 degrees S, 150 degrees E.

 Continue south for a scuba adventure through the Great Barrier Reef, 20 degrees S, 150 degrees E. G'day mate!

BONUS: The International Date Line is a longitudinal line that divides one day from another. If you cross this line moving east, it is a full day earlier. Moving westward across the line, it is a full day later. If you sail from California to Australia, would you move forward or back a day as you crossed the dateline?

Now add this sticker to your map!

Wise Words

Fill in the missing commas and quotation marks.

Quotation Marks

The writer Isak Dinesen once said The cure for anything is saltwater—sweat, tears, or the sea.

The captain pointed upward and said Red sky at night, sailors' delight; red sky at morning, sailors take warning.

I patted my brother on the back and said Well, there are plenty of other fish in the sea.

The shark poster said Reading is jawsome!

The mermaid advised Marlin Just keep swimming!

How inappropriate to call this planet Earth wrote Arthur C. Clarke when it is clearly Ocean.

Poet Anne Stevenson wrote The sea is as near as we come to another world.

Remember said the nature guide sand dollars are living creatures, not souvenirs.

Grandma always says Wait an hour after eating to go swimming.

Upon completion, add these stickers to your path on the map!

Brain Box

Quotation marks indicate dialogue or show what a person has said. Place quotation marks before the first word and after the ending punctuation of each quotation. Place a comma and space before a quotation that begins midsentence. Place a comma before the quotation mark when the quotation ends midsentence.

All Aboard the SS *Simple*

Read about the different simple machines. Then draw a line to match each machine with the correct cargo box.

Simple Machines

An **inclined plane** is a flat surface that slopes up or down. It makes it easier to roll objects up or down.

A **lever** is a rod or bar that turns on a point known as the fulcrum. It is used to lift, move, or pry open things by applying pressure to them.

A **pulley** is a grooved wheel over which a rope can hang. An object can be fastened to one side of the rope. By pulling on the other side, you can lift that object.

A **wedge** is an object with a thick end and thin end, so that two of the sides form a triangle. It can be used to split or slice something.

A **wheel** is a round object that turns on a rod called an axle. Together, they are known as the wheel and axle.

A **screw** is actually a long inclined plane wrapped around a rod. It is used to move things up or down. In the case of small metal screws, it is the screw that moves up and down.

Upon completion, add this sticker to your path on the map!

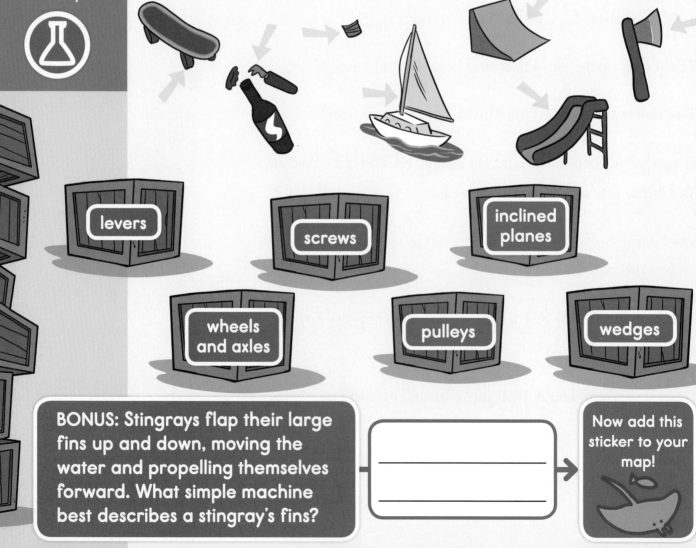

levers

screws

inclined planes

wheels and axles

pulleys

wedges

BONUS: Stingrays flap their large fins up and down, moving the water and propelling themselves forward. What simple machine best describes a stingray's fins?

Now add this sticker to your map!

Level 3A complete!

Add this achievement sticker to your path...

...and move on to

Level 4A

on page 48!

...OR GO ON AN OUTSIDE QUEST AND MOVE ON TO LEVEL 4B ON PAGE 58!

Lobster Riddle

Multiply using place value. Find the products.
Then use your answers to decode the riddle on the next page.

Multi-Digit
Multiplication

START
LEVEL
3B
HERE!

T
```
   33
 × 6
 ────
   18  ← 6 × 3
+ 180  ← 6 × 30
```

H
```
   127
 ×   2
 ─────
    14  ← 2 × 7
    40  ← 2 × 20
 + 200  ← 2 × 100
```

L
```
2,345
 × 3
```

I
```
3,242
  × 3
```

B
```
 60
× 60
```

C
```
417
× 4
```

P
```
651
× 3
```

G
```
856
× 5
```

O
```
76
× 9
```

S
```
64
× 5
```

D
```
2,316
  × 4
```

W
```
78
× 2
```

E

```
    78
  × 24
  ─────
    32  ← 4 × 8
   280  ← 4 × 70
   160  ← 20 × 8
 + 1400 ← 20 × 70
  ─────
```

Multi-Digit Multiplication

Upon completion, add these stickers to your path on the map!

U

```
  467
 ×  4
 ─────
```

R

```
  170
 ×  9
 ─────
```

F

```
   48
 × 53
 ─────
```

A

```
   19
 × 22
 ─────
```

Why is the fisherman afraid of lobsters?

3,600	1,872	1,668	418	1,868	320	1,872

| 254 | 1,872 | | 9,726 | 320 | | 1,668 | 7,035 | 418 | 156 | 320 |

| 198 | 1,530 | 684 | 1,953 | 254 | 684 | 3,600 | 9,726 | 1,668 |

State
Abbreviations

Name That State!

Study the map and answer each question. Write the full names of the states in your answers.

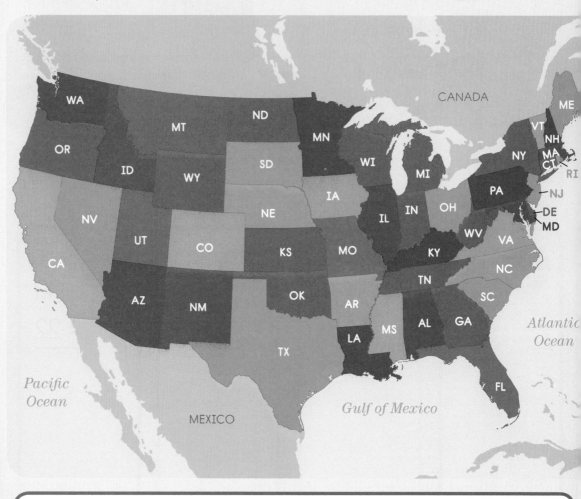

Upon completion, add this sticker to your path on the map!

Which five states have coastline on the Gulf of Mexico?

_____

Which states, known as the Four Corners States, come together at a single point?

_____

Which states share a border with Texas?

_____

Missouri shares its border with a whopping eight states. So does one other state. What is it?

_____

Which state shares its border with just one state?

_____

Factor Feast

Color each bubble that has a factor of the whale's number.
Then circle the whales whose numbers are prime numbers.

Factors,
Multiples, and
Primes

Upon
completion,
add this
sticker to
your path on
the map!

Remainders
and Word
Problems

Exploring Under the Sea

Solve each word problem. Then draw a line to match each answer to the correct answer description.

An undersea exploration pod has enough room for 3 people. How many pods are needed if 14 scientists are exploring under the sea at the same time?

The answer is the **quotient only.**

The scientists collected 46 fish. The fish were placed in tanks that hold 6 fish each. How many fish were in the tank that was not full?

The answer is the **remainder only.**

Each scientist's bucket holds 8 pounds of sediment. The scientists tested 70 pounds of sediment. How many full buckets did they have?

The answer is the **quotient + 1.**

Each sightseeing boat can carry 9 people. If there is only one boat and 57 people want to ride, how many trips will the boat have to make?

Upon completion, add this sticker to your path on the map!

Brain Box

$14 \div 3 = 4\ r2$

or

$$3\ \overline{)\ 14}\ \ ^{4\ r2}$$

14 is the dividend

4 is the quotient

2 is the remainder

3 is the divisor

Catch of the Day

Fill in each blank with the correct conjunction from the box. Use each word only once.

Conjunctions

and	or	unless	while	however
but	so	although	because	

"I heard you have the freshest lobster on the wharf _____ the cheesiest grits around."

"We do have the freshest lobster, _____ we sold out of it."

"Then I'll have the catch of the day, a side of grits, and fried green tomatoes, _____ I'm very hungry."

"Would you like a bottle of water _____ root beer _____ you wait?"

"I'll take root beer, _____ it has caffeine."

"It does not, so here you go. And here are your scuba gear and net."

"Scuba gear? Net? _____ I love to scuba dive, I came here to eat, not swim."

"Well, our fisherman is out sick, _____ if you want the catch of the day, you have to catch it."

"Fine. I will catch the lobster. _____, I only *eat* fresh seafood. I hope that I'm not expected to *cook* it, too."

Brain Box

A **conjunction** is a word used to link phrases, clauses, or sentences.

BONUS: Write a sentence about a deep-sea anglerfish that includes a conjunction.

_____
_____
_____
_____

Now add this sticker to your map!

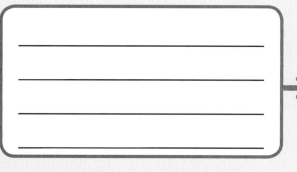

Waves
and Wave
Properties

Catch a Wave

Read about waves. Then complete the crossword puzzle.

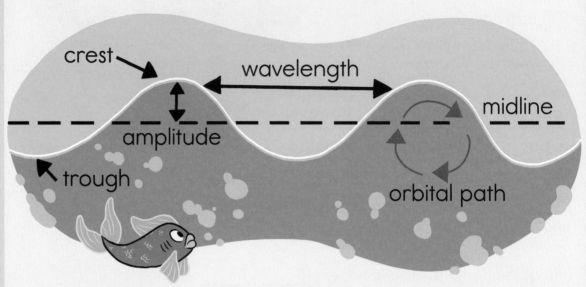

A wave is the movement of energy in a regular pattern. Waves can move through a medium, such as water (an ocean wave) or air (a sound wave). Though the wave transports energy from place to place, it does not transport the matter through which it moves. Instead, the particles simply vibrate at different speeds in place. For instance, even though ocean waves move across the water, the water particles themselves only travel in tiny circles in place.

Waves are measured in several ways. Wavelength is the length of a full cycle of a wave. It can be measured from crest (high point) to crest, or trough (low point) to trough. Amplitude is the height of the wave from its midline to its crest. Frequency is the number of complete waves that pass a single point in one second.

There are two main types of waves. Ocean waves are transverse waves. These waves move at a right angle to the direction of the vibration of the particles. As water particles bob up and down, the wave moves across.

Sound waves are longitudinal waves. They move along the same direction as the vibration of particles. As the air particles vibrate side to side, the sound wave also moves back and forth—like a Slinky!

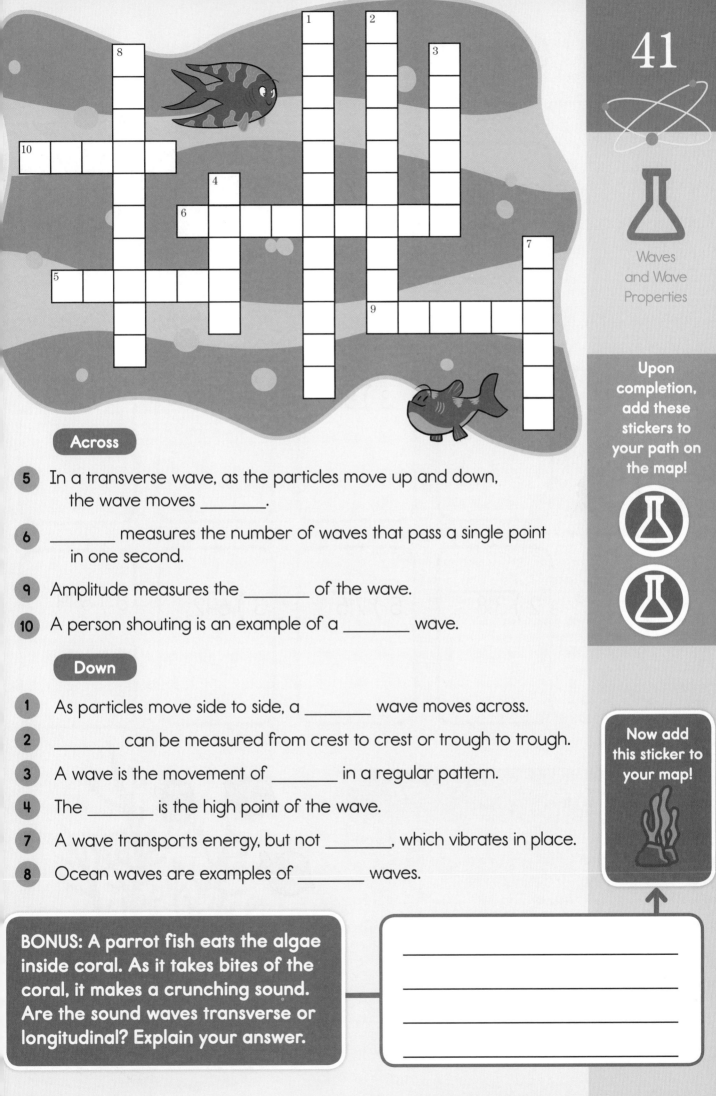

Across

5 In a transverse wave, as the particles move up and down, the wave moves _____.

6 _____ measures the number of waves that pass a single point in one second.

9 Amplitude measures the _____ of the wave.

10 A person shouting is an example of a _____ wave.

Down

1 As particles move side to side, a _____ wave moves across.

2 _____ can be measured from crest to crest or trough to trough.

3 A wave is the movement of _____ in a regular pattern.

4 The _____ is the high point of the wave.

7 A wave transports energy, but not _____, which vibrates in place.

8 Ocean waves are examples of _____ waves.

Upon completion, add these stickers to your path on the map!

Now add this sticker to your map!

BONUS: A parrot fish eats the algae inside coral. As it takes bites of the coral, it makes a crunching sound. Are the sound waves transverse or longitudinal? Explain your answer.

_____

_____

_____

_____

Long Division

Coral Reef Division

Divide to find the quotient and remainder, if any.

$8\overline{)96}$

$4\overline{)64}$

$5\overline{)95}$

$3\overline{)84}$

$6\overline{)90}$

$9\overline{)909}$

$2\overline{)318}$

$5\overline{)715}$

$3\overline{)642}$

$8\overline{)899}$

Brain Box

When dividing a 3-digit number by a 1-digit number:

Example:

$$\begin{array}{r} 195\ r1 \\ 4\overline{)781} \\ -4 \\ \hline 38 \\ -36 \\ \hline 21 \\ -20 \\ \hline 1 \end{array}$$

Step 1: Divide into the hundreds.

Step 2: Subtract.

Step 3: Bring down the tens and then divide into the tens.

Step 4: Subtract again.

Step 5: Bring down the ones and divide into the ones.

Step 6: If there is a remainder, write it next to the answer.

Solve each word problem.

If there are 84 firefish hiding in 7 different crevices of the reef with the same number in each, how many firefish are in each crevice?

Long Division

6 trumpet fish eat 216 gobies. If each trumpet fish sucked in the same number of gobies, how many gobies did each trumpet fish eat?

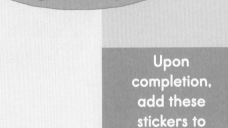

Peacock flounders have 2 eyes on the same side of their flat bodies. If you see 74 eyes resting on coral, how many flounders is that?

Upon completion, add these stickers to your path on the map!

There were 135 parrotfish sleeping in 5 equal groups in protected areas of the reef. How many parrotfish were sleeping in each area?

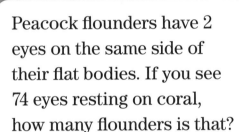

If 3 clownfish share 912 plankton equally, how many plankton does each clownfish eat?

Now add this sticker to your map!

BONUS: Starfish have an eye at the end of each of their 5 arms. If there are 95 eyes in a group of starfish, how many starfish are in the group?

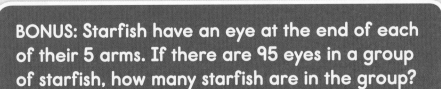

Local, State, and Federal Governments

Mermaid Government

Like the United States of America, the United States of Mermaids has federal, state, and local governments. Read about each government. Then write which level of government should be responsible for each problem.

The federal government makes laws for the country. It negotiates with other mermaid countries. It is also responsible for building a national military, building waterways that go through multiple states, and collecting income taxes.

A state government makes laws for that state only. It is also responsible for the state police, state education standards, state sales tax, and state waterways.

A local government can govern a county, town, city, and/or school district. It makes and enforces laws for that small area. It is responsible for the fire department, local police, trash collection, parks and recreation, and local school districts.

Shipwreck Park in Coral City has several broken slides. Who should fix them?

_____

Sharkansas's Waterway 62 has become crowded and needs more lanes. Who should rebuild the waterway?

_____

Planktown needs a new elementary school. Who should build it?

_____

It's time for all mermaids to pay their income taxes. Who should collect the taxes?

_____

The state of New Fishire is in debt and may raise the state sales tax. Who can authorize this?

_____

Mermaindy has declared war on the United States of Mermaids. Who will lead the military in this war?

_____

BONUS: If scuba divers were taking coral from the reef of the United States of Mermaids as souvenirs, what could the local, state, or federal government do to stop this?

_____

_____

_____

45

Local, State, and Federal Governments

Upon completion, add these stickers to your path on the map!

Now add this sticker to your map!

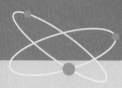

Spelling

Pop It!

Study each spelling word. Then cover the word and write it correctly in the bubble. If you get it right, you can "pop" the bubble by putting a checkmark through it.

Upon completion, add this sticker to your path on the map!

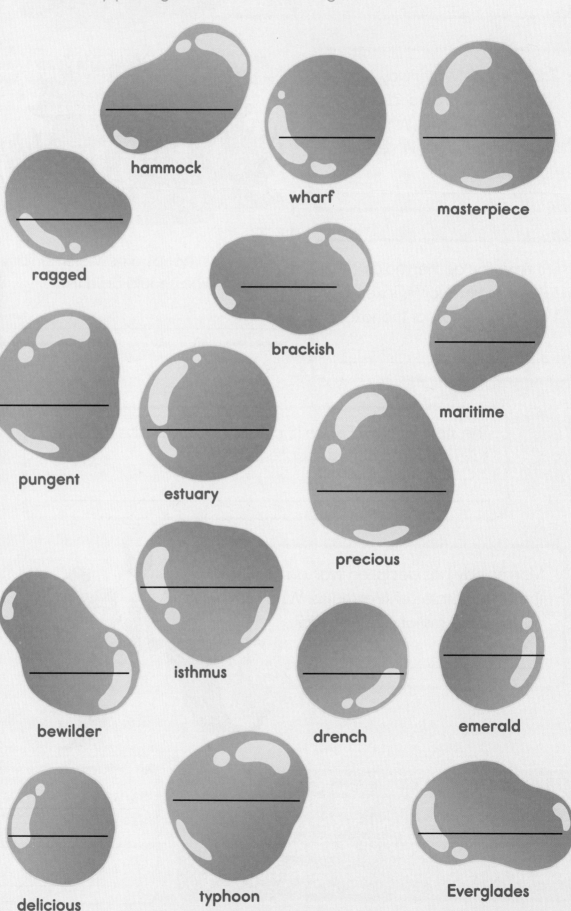

hammock

wharf

masterpiece

ragged

brackish

maritime

pungent

estuary

precious

bewilder

isthmus

drench

emerald

delicious

typhoon

Everglades

Level 3B complete!

Add this achievement sticker to your path…

… AND GO ON AN OUTSIDE QUEST AND MOVE ON TO LEVEL 4A ON PAGE 48!

… or move on to

Level 4B

on page 58!

Greek and
Latin Prefixes
and Suffixes

**START
LEVEL
4A
HERE!**

The Life Aquatic

Read the meaning of each Greek and Latin prefix and suffix.
Then fill in each blank with the correct prefix or suffix.

aqua-
Latin: water

-meter
Greek: (*metron*)
measure

audi-
Latin: to hear

ambi-
Latin: around or
both

photo-
Greek: (*phos*) light

astro-
Greek: (*astron*)
a star

amphi-
Greek: both

aero-
Greek: (*aer*) air

-ology
Greek: (*logia*)
speech; now
means to study

tele-
Greek: far off

-phobia
Greek: (*phobos*)
fear

anti-
Greek: opposed

Aunt Amphitrite's _____bious car could be driven on both land and water.

Poseidon filled the _____rium with salt water and gently set the anemone inside.

After dramatically hurling his cell phone into the ocean, Julius had to use a _____phone to call his brother Marcus overseas.

A day at the beach was no picnic for Odysseus; he had developed thalasso_____—fear of the ocean.

Triton studied overfishing for his master's degree in marine bi_____.

Like all plants, seaweed needs sunlight for _____synthesis.

The thermo_____ measured the frigid ocean temperature.

Cicero looked around the café and said, "The food isn't any good, but the _____ence is nice."

Upon completion, add these stickers to your path on the map!

Brain Box

Many English prefixes and suffixes come from Greek and Latin words. Knowing what these suffixes and prefixes mean can help you decode the meanings of unfamiliar words.

Upon completion, add this sticker to your path on the map!

The First 13

Read about the original U.S. colonies. Using clues from the text, color the northern colonies **red**, the middle colonies **orange**, and the southern colonies **blue**.

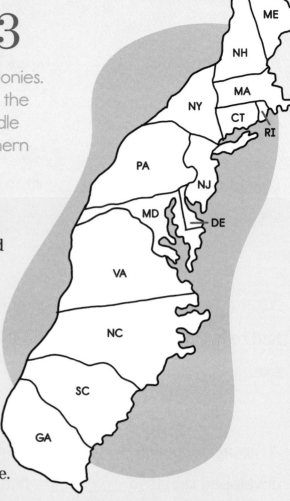

Puritans settled in the **northern colonies** of New England to build communities that would glorify God. These colonies had a strict religious culture. Economically, the region specialized in shipbuilding, and in mills and factories, which were powered by water along the coast. Small farms dotted the region, but towns were the center of life here.

In contrast, the **southern colonies**, the northernmost of which was Maryland, were founded for economic gain. The rich soil was ideal for cash crops such as rice, tobacco, and indigo. Slavery existed in all colonies. However, in the South, slave labor allowed landowners to farm large swaths of land and become wealthy. Meanwhile, the slaves endured deplorable poverty and horrible treatment. Many plantations were self-sufficient, and towns were few and far between.

The **middle colonies**, the northernmost of which was New York, had a combination of farms and towns. With a more moderate climate than New England, it was better suited for grain and livestock. Because of the rich soil, small and large farms flourished. The middle colonies were well situated for trade among the colonies, and port cities arose along the coast. Here, settlers arrived from many walks of life.

BONUS: Prior to the construction of railroads and highways, why might it have been beneficial for the 13 colonies to have access to the Atlantic Ocean?

_____

_____

_____

_____

_____

→ Now add this sticker to your map!

All About Oceans

Find the capitalization mistakes. Draw three lines under letters that should be capitalized. Draw a diagonal line through letters that should not be capitalized.

Capitalization

The pacific ocean is the largest and the deepest of the five world oceans.

Cold Ocean water is more nutrient-rich than warm ocean water, resulting in more sea life.

Storms off the coast of portugal can create massive waves, like the 100-foot one surfed by world record holder garrett mcnamara.

Penguins are often paired with polar bears in illustrations; but in fact, polar bears swim in the arctic ocean, and penguins in the antarctic ocean.

The phytoplankton and zooplankton in cold water make it look murky, whereas warm water is often Crystal clear.

The fastest fish in the ocean is the Sailfish, which has been clocked at 68 miles per hour.

Visit Vaadhoo Island, near india, and you may see the ocean glowing bright blue because of bioluminescent phytoplankton.

Upon completion, add this sticker to your path on the map!

Brain Box

Capitalize: the names of people, places (such as buildings, schools, towns, countries, continents, rivers, and mountains) and things; the titles that come before people's names, as in Dr. Flood or Professor Plum; and the days of the week and the months of the year.

Do not capitalize: words such as school, river, mountain, or doctor, unless they are part of proper names; Example: Sharkansas Elementary School.

Equivalent
Fractions

Pool Part-y

Write the equivalent fraction
and shade parts of the pools
to show equivalent fractions.

$$\frac{1}{2} = \frac{\square}{\square}$$

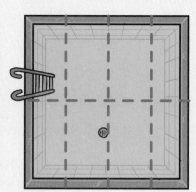

$$\frac{2}{3} = \frac{\square}{\square}$$

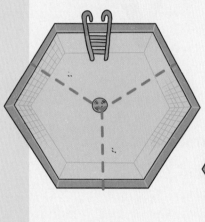

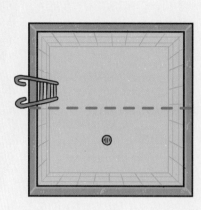

$$\frac{5}{6} = \frac{\square}{\square}$$

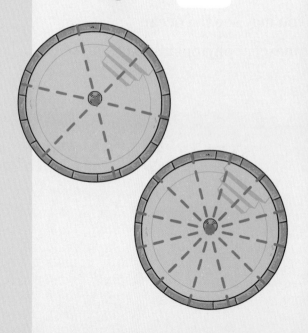

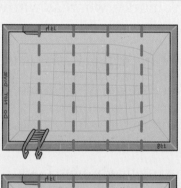

$$\frac{3}{5} = \frac{\square}{\square}$$

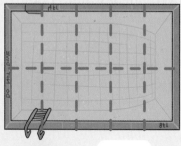

Fill in the boxes to show equivalent fractions.

Equivalent
Fractions

$$\frac{1}{3} = \frac{}{6} = \frac{}{12}$$

$$\frac{1}{4} = \frac{}{8} = \frac{}{12}$$

$$\frac{1}{2} = \frac{}{4} = \frac{}{6} = \frac{}{8} = \frac{}{10} = \frac{}{12}$$

Upon completion, add these stickers to your path on the map!

BONUS: One-fifth of the pool toys were inflatable seahorses. Write $\frac{1}{5}$ as an equivalent fraction with 10 as the denominator.

Now add this sticker to your map!

Ocean, Sea, Open Water

Use clues from the thesaurus and dictionary entries to replace the given word with one of the synonyms provided.

Thesaurus

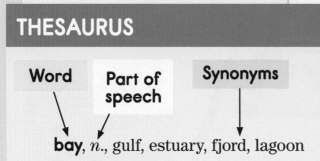

THESAURUS

Word   **Part of speech**   **Synonyms**

bay, *n.*, gulf, estuary, fjord, lagoon

Boat, *n.*, canoe, sloop, yacht

Fisherman, *n.*, angler, fisher, sailor, seaman

Rough, *adj.*, choppy, shaggy

Shore, *n.*, beach, lakeside, seaside

Swim, *v.*, float, glide, paddle

DICTIONARY

Word   **Pronounciation**   **Definition**

Part of speech

angler, \'aŋ-glər\, *n.* a fisherman who uses a rod and line

choppy \'chä-pē\ *adj.* rough with small waves

estuary \'es-chə-'wer-ē, 'esh-\ *n.* a water passage where the tide meets a river current; esp: an arm of the sea at the lower end of a river

fjord \fē-'ȯrd, 'fē-; 'fyȯrd\ *n.* a narrow inlet of the sea between cliffs or steep slopes

lagoon \lə-'gün\ *n.* a shallow sound, channel, or pond near a larger body of water

paddle \'pa-dᵊl\ *v.* to move one's arms or feet through the water

shaggy \'sha-gē\ *adj.* covered with or consisting of long, coarse, or matted hair

sloop \'slüp\ *n.* a sailboat with one mast and a single jib

yacht \'yät\ *n.* a large recreational boat or watercraft

Thesaurus

Living by Lake Michigan, Rosie often spent her Saturdays at the **shore** seaside lakeside _____.

As the storm approached, the captain ordered the **boat's** yacht's sloop's _____ single sail to be furled.

The sailors felt queasy as the ship sailed through **rough** shaggy choppy _____ waters.

As she sailed through the **bay** fjord lagoon _____, L'Shay imagined the glaciers that formed such dramatic cliffs.

The three-time Ironwoman champion **swam** paddled floated _____ furiously toward the shore.

As freshwater from a river mingles with salt water from the ocean, the **bay** estuary fjord _____ is filled with nutrients that feed an array of animals.

When they weren't sailing, the Widmore family motored through Europe on their **boat** sloop yacht _____.

The pirate's fancy shirt and jacket were overshadowed by his tangled hair and **rough** choppy shaggy _____ beard.

With each swish of her tail, the mermaid **swam** glided paddled _____ effortlessly through the water.

Upon completion, add these stickers to your path on the map!

Brain Box

A **thesaurus** can be used to find **synonyms** for words. However, synonyms can have slightly different meanings, so one cannot always be substituted for another. A **dictionary** can be used to find the exact definition of each word.

Earth, Sun,
and Moon

**Upon
completion,
add this
sticker to
your path on
the map!**

Brain
Box

Earth's
relationship
to the objects
upon it, and
to the sun
and moon,
causes many
phenomena
that can be
observed in
everyday life.
These include
day, nighttime,
the seasons,
and the tides.

Worldwide Wonders

Draw a line to match each caption
with the correct illustration.

When the earth revolves
on its axis, about half of it
faces away from the sun,
resulting in night.

The sun is a star like many
others, but appears larger
because it is closer to Earth.

The moon also has a
gravitational pull. It pulls the
ocean toward it, resulting in
high tide.

Earth has a tilted axis. When
the Northern Hemisphere
is tilted toward the sun, it is
summer there (and winter in
the Southern Hemisphere).

Large objects such as Earth
have gravity, which pulls
objects toward them. So,
"falling down" is actually
falling toward Earth.

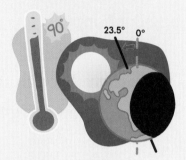

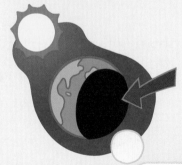

**BONUS: Write a sentence
about a seal experiencing
one of the phenomena
described above.**

_____
_____
_____

**Now add
this sticker
to your
map!**

Level 4A complete!

Add this achievement sticker to your path…

…and move on to

Level 5A

on page 68!

…or move on to

Level 5B

on page 82!

Comparing
Fractions

START
LEVEL
4B
HERE!

Squid Ink

Fill in each missing fraction on the number line. (HINT: Use $\frac{1}{2}$ as a benchmark to fill in the correct fractions.)

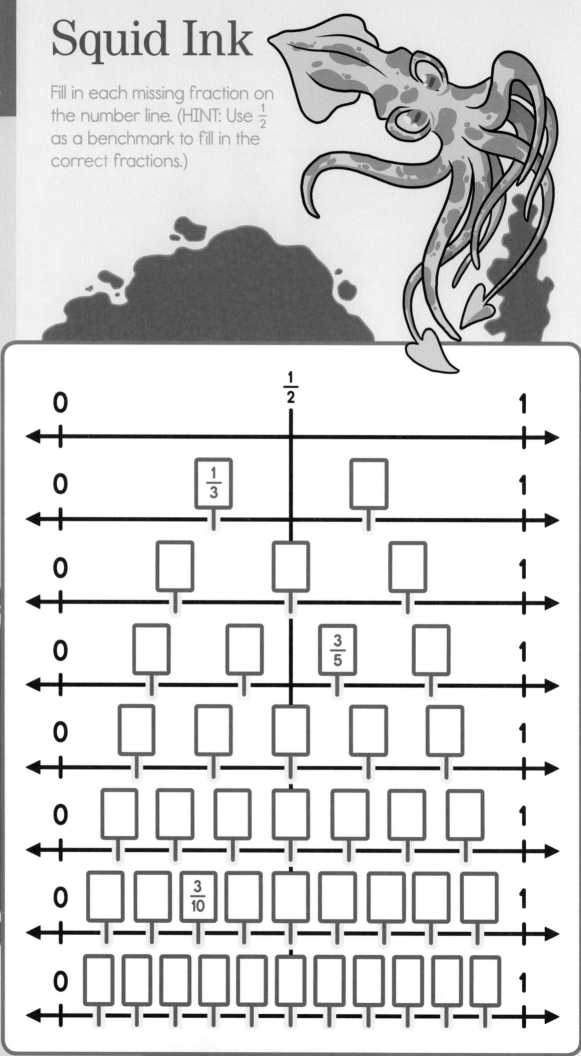

Use the number line on page 58 to circle the correct relationships between the fractions.

Use the number line on page 58

$\frac{1}{4} < \frac{4}{8}$

$\frac{1}{4} > \frac{4}{8}$

$\frac{1}{4} = \frac{4}{8}$

Comparing Fractions

$\frac{2}{3} < \frac{2}{5}$

$\frac{2}{3} = \frac{2}{5}$

$\frac{2}{3} > \frac{2}{5}$

$\frac{5}{8} < \frac{2}{5}$

$\frac{5}{8} = \frac{2}{5}$

$\frac{5}{8} > \frac{2}{5}$

Upon completion, add these stickers to your path on the map!

$\frac{7}{10} < \frac{5}{12}$

$\frac{7}{10} = \frac{5}{12}$

$\frac{7}{10} > \frac{5}{12}$

$\frac{4}{5} < \frac{3}{8}$

$\frac{4}{5} > \frac{3}{8}$

$\frac{4}{5} = \frac{3}{8}$

$\frac{2}{5} < \frac{5}{6}$

$\frac{2}{5} = \frac{5}{6}$

$\frac{2}{5} > \frac{5}{6}$

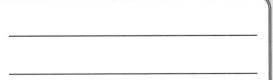

Which is greater: $\frac{5}{8}$ ounces of squid ink or $\frac{4}{12}$ ounces of squid ink? Explain how you know your answer.

_____

_____

_____

_____

It Starts with the Sun

Read about the food chain. Then complete the diagram by drawing the missing items.

Food Chain

Upon completion, add this sticker to your path on the map!

A food chain is a series of organisms, each of which feeds on the previous one. Every food chain relies on the sun's energy. Plants turn the energy (along with carbon dioxide, water, and nutrients) into carbohydrates in a process called photosynthesis. When animals eat the plants, the carbohydrates provide them with the energy to live.

In an ocean, tiny plants called phytoplankton photosynthesize by absorbing energy from the sun and carbon dioxide and nutrients from the water. The phytoplankton are then eaten by tiny animals called zooplankton, which in turn are eaten by larger animals, such as shrimp. The shrimp are eaten by larger animals still—tuna, for instance. Finally, the tuna is eaten by an animal at the top of the food chain, in this case, a great white shark. Each eaten animal provides needed energy for the predator.

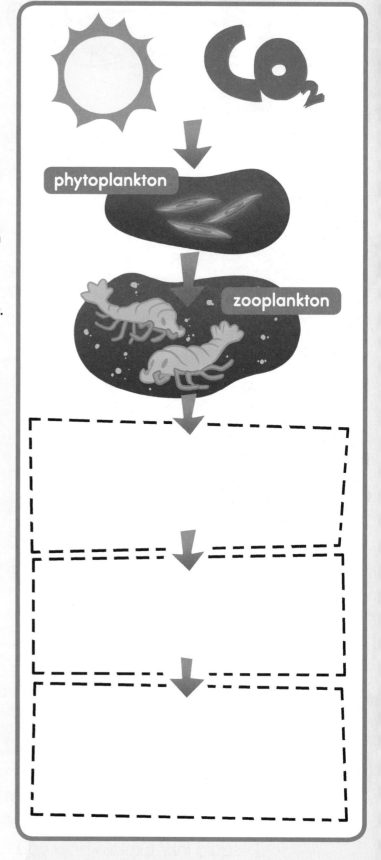

Map Master

Use the clues, filling in the world map with the names of
the seven continents and five world oceans.

Geography

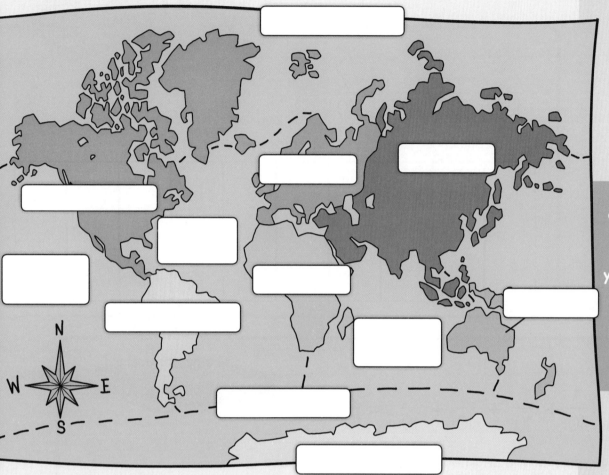

Upon
completion,
add this
sticker to
your path on
the map!

Africa and Europe lie east of the Atlantic Ocean.

Asia, the largest continent, is east of Europe and Africa.

The Indian Ocean is in the middle of Africa, Asia, and Australia.

North America lies between the Pacific Ocean to the west and the
Atlantic Ocean to the east.

South America is connected to North America by a narrow isthmus.

Antarctica is the southernmost continent and is surrounded by the
Antarctic Ocean.

Australia is sometimes called the "island continent."

The Arctic Ocean spans the North Pole.

Segmented Worms

Write numbers in the equations to make the sum $\frac{7}{10}$. Then color the segments in different colors to match your equation.

$$\frac{\boxed{}}{10} + \frac{\boxed{}}{10} + \frac{\boxed{}}{10} = \frac{7}{10}$$

Now color the segments using 3 colors to make $\frac{7}{10}$.

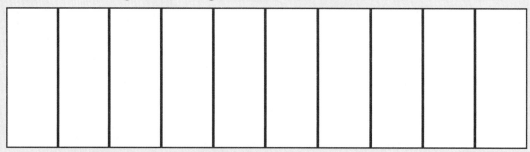

$$\frac{1}{10} + \frac{\boxed{}}{10} + \frac{\boxed{}}{10} + \frac{\boxed{}}{10} = \frac{7}{10}$$

Now color the segments using 4 colors to make $\frac{7}{10}$.

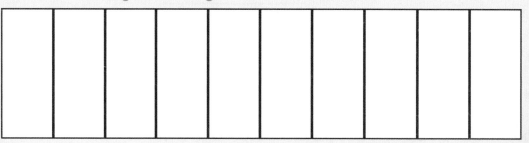

$$\frac{1}{10} + \frac{\boxed{}}{10} + \frac{\boxed{}}{10} + \frac{\boxed{}}{10} + \frac{\boxed{}}{10} = \frac{7}{10}$$

Now color the segments using 5 colors to make $\frac{7}{10}$.

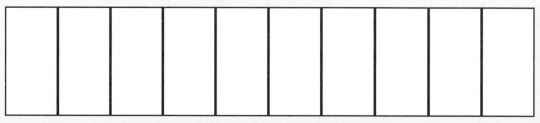

Write equations to show different ways to make the sum $\frac{7}{8}$.
Color the segments to match.

Decompose Fractions

$$\frac{7}{8} =$$

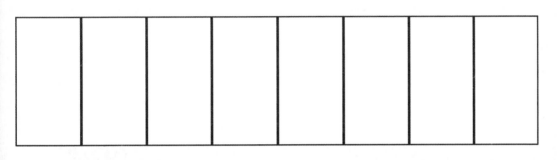

$$\frac{7}{8} =$$

Upon completion, add these stickers to your path on the map!

Together these segments show $\frac{8}{6}$. Write the equation that shows how the segments make the sum $\frac{8}{6}$.

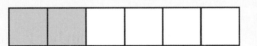

$$\frac{8}{6} =$$

Now add this sticker to your map!

BONUS: A lobster eats 2 whole sea worms. Color the segments using different colors to show the different bites the lobster took. Then write the fractions.

$$2 = \frac{10}{5} =$$

Similes and Metaphors

Upon completion, add this sticker to your path on the map!

Brain Box

A **simile** is a comparison that includes the words **like** or **as**. Example: quiet as a mouse. A **metaphor** is a comparison that does not include "like" or "as." Example: Francie was a beast on the basketball court.

Like a Boss

Underline the simile or metaphor in each sentence. Write an S on the line if it is a simile and an M if it is a metaphor.

Cleaning out the garage seemed as daunting as counting the grains of sand on the beach. _____

Everyone knew David was bullying Chris, but when it came to being suspended, David was as slippery as an eel. _____

In the lemonade-stand business, Ceresa was a real shark. _____

By the end of lessons, Luke could swim like a fish. _____

Sea lions are the dogs of the sea. _____

Cora's dream of a beach vacation was like a mermaid: lovely but not real. _____

After placing second in her surfing competition, Wendy cried an ocean of tears. _____

Choose one of the similes or metaphors from above, and write its literal meaning.

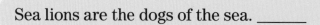

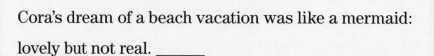

_____

_____

_____

Float Like an Otter, Sting Like a Jellyfish

Rewrite the similes so that they relate to the ocean.

Similes and Metaphors

as hungry as a bear → as hungry as a shark

as fast as light _____

as big as a house _____

as cute as a button _____

as quiet as a mouse _____

as smart as a whip _____

as cool as the other
side of the pillow _____

as cold as ice _____

as cool as a cucumber _____

as quick as a whistle _____

as strong as an ox _____

Upon completion, add this sticker to your path on the map!

BONUS: Complete the simile about a seashell.

As _____ as a seashell →

Now add this sticker to your map!

Mimic Octopus

Convert each fraction to mixed number form.

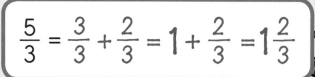

$$\frac{5}{3} = \frac{3}{3} + \frac{2}{3} = 1 + \frac{2}{3} = 1\frac{2}{3}$$

$$\frac{11}{5} = \frac{}{5} + \frac{}{5} + \frac{}{5} = $$

Mixed
Numbers

$$\frac{7}{4} = \frac{}{4} + \frac{}{4} = $$

$$\frac{10}{3} = \frac{}{3} + $$

Upon
completion,
add this
sticker to
your path on
the map!

$$\frac{20}{8} = \frac{}{8} + $$

Convert each mixed number to an improper fraction.

$$1\frac{1}{4} = \frac{4}{4} + \frac{1}{4} = \frac{5}{4}$$

$$1\frac{7}{12} = $$

$$2\frac{3}{10} = \frac{}{10} + \frac{}{10} + \frac{}{10} = $$

$$3\frac{5}{8} = $$

$$2\frac{3}{4} = $$

Level 4B complete!

Add this achievement sticker to your path...

...and move on to

Level 5A

on page 68!

...or
move on to

Level 5B

on page 82!

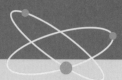

Add and
Subtract
Fractions

START
LEVEL
5A
HERE!

Upon
completion,
add this
sticker to
your path on
the map!

Puffin Chicks

Add or subtract the fractions.
Draw a line to match each question
with a puffin with the correct answer.

$$\frac{5}{12} + \frac{4}{12} =$$

$$\frac{3}{5} - \frac{1}{5} =$$

$$\frac{3}{8} + \frac{4}{8} =$$

$$\frac{4}{5} - \frac{1}{5} =$$

$$\frac{6}{8} + \frac{7}{8} =$$

$\frac{7}{8}$

$\frac{2}{5}$

$\frac{13}{8}$

$\frac{9}{12}$

$\frac{3}{5}$

Brain Box

To add fractions with like
denominators, add the
numerators. Use the same
denominator.

$$\frac{2}{6} + \frac{3}{6} = \frac{2+3}{6} = \frac{5}{6}$$

To subtract fractions with
like denominators, subtract
the numerators. Use the
same denominator.

$$\frac{7}{8} - \frac{2}{8} = \frac{7-2}{8} = \frac{5}{8}$$

Howlin' at the Moon

Study the diagram. Then answer the questions.

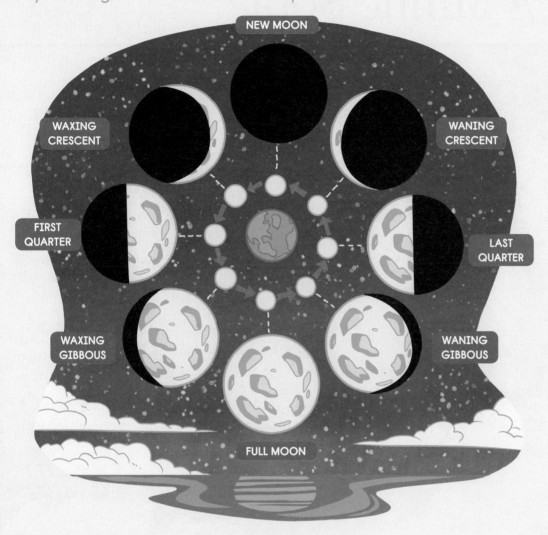

NEW MOON

WAXING CRESCENT

WANING CRESCENT

FIRST QUARTER

LAST QUARTER

WAXING GIBBOUS

WANING GIBBOUS

FULL MOON

Can you see the same amount of the moon during the first quarter and last quarter?

_____

During which period can you see more moon—during a waning gibbous moon or a waning crescent moon?

_____

Based on the context, what might gibbous mean?

| hollowed out | swollen on one side | in the shadows |

Which of the following explains why the moon is not visible from Earth during the new moon?

The sun lights the moon on the side that we can see.

The sun lights the moon on the side that we cannot see.

Brain Box

Lunar, or moon, phases refer to the portion of the moon that can be viewed from Earth. The moon cycles through its phases in 29.5 days, which is the amount of time it takes the moon to revolve around Earth.

What Did Missis Sip?
A Minne Sota

Study the physical map.
Then answer the questions.

Physical Maps

Upon completion, add this sticker to your path on the map!

Where are the Mississippi River's headwaters (i.e., the start of the river)?

_____

Into which large body of water does the Mississippi River empty?

_____

Name the major Mississippi River tributary that begins in Colorado.

_____

If you cross the Mississippi River from Arkansas, which two states might you enter?

_____

The Mississippi River runs along the borders of which 10 states? _____

_____

The Great White North

Read each sentence. Use context clues to write an approximate definition of the bold word.

During the Ice Age, **glaciers** flowed farther south, carrying sediment and even large boulders.

_____

_____

There are only two expanses of ice large enough to be classified as **ice sheets**: one in Greenland and the other in Antarctica.

_____

_____

As the **permafrost** melted, the thawing soil sank, and the house collapsed.

_____

_____

Ships traveling across the Arctic Ocean must beware of **icebergs** floating nearby.

_____

Vocabulary

Upon completion, add this sticker to your path on the map!

Now write the bolded word below its definition.

ice that extends on land for at least 20,000 square miles (50,000 square kilometers) _____

a layer of soil beneath the surface that remains frozen _____

a river of ice that is slowly moving under its own weight _____

ice that has broken off from a glacier and is floating in the water _____

Operations Ahoy!

Use equivalent fractions to add and subtract mixed numbers.
Find the sum or difference.

Adding and
Subtracting
Mixed
Numbers

$2\frac{1}{4} + 1\frac{3}{4} = \frac{}{4} + \frac{}{4} = \frac{}{4} = $

$3\frac{1}{3} + 1\frac{2}{3} = \frac{}{3} + \frac{}{3} = \frac{}{3} = $

$4\frac{2}{5} - \frac{4}{5} = \frac{}{5} - \frac{}{5} = \frac{}{5} = $

$1\frac{4}{10} + 1\frac{9}{10} = \frac{}{10} + \frac{}{10} = \frac{}{10} = $

$3\frac{2}{6} - 1\frac{5}{6} = \frac{}{6} - \frac{}{6} = \frac{}{6} = $

Your friend makes a sail using $1\frac{1}{8}$-meter-long cloth. You make a smaller sail with a $\frac{5}{8}$-meter-long cloth. How many meters shorter in length is your sail?

_____ meters

Adding and Subtracting Mixed Numbers

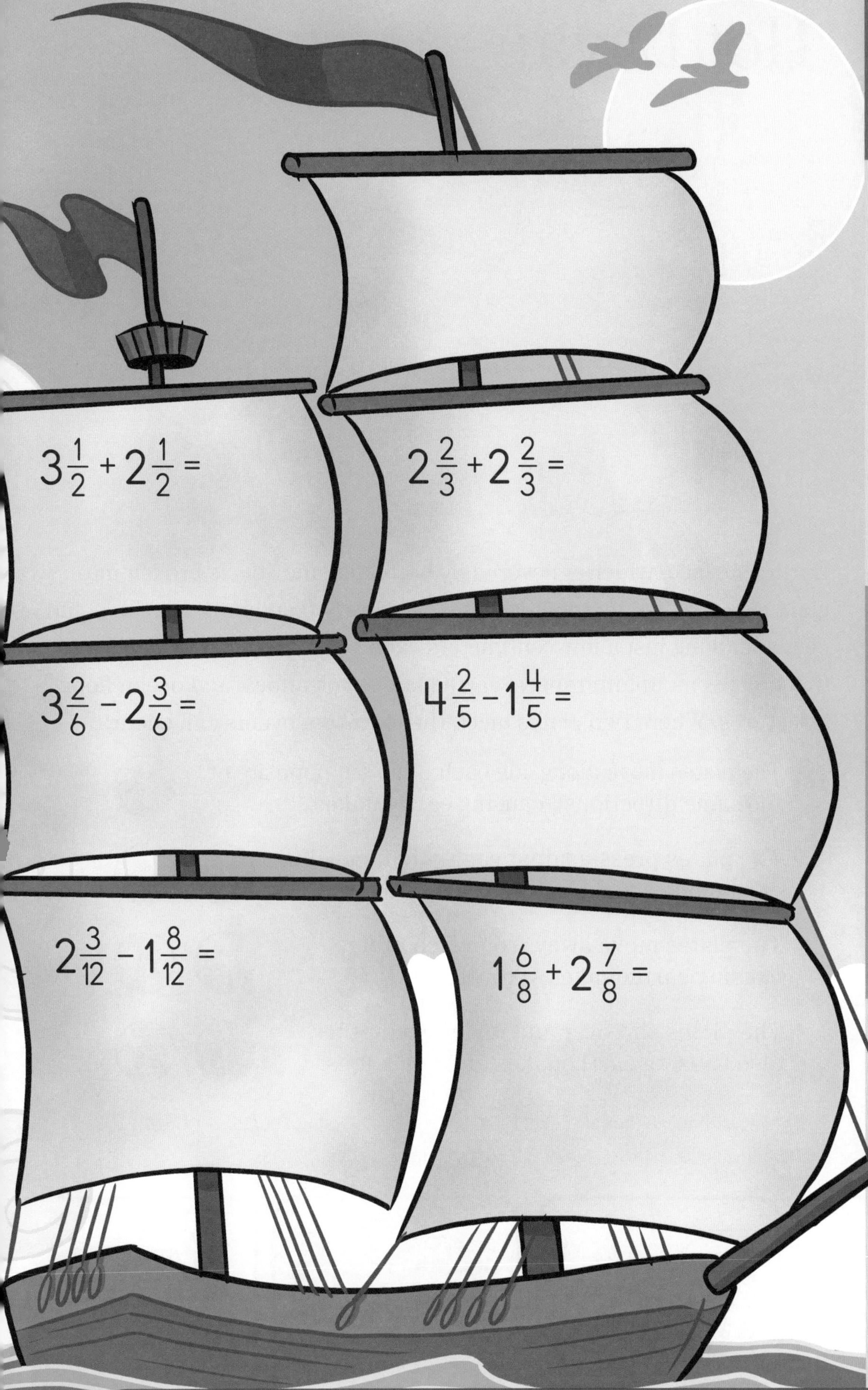

$3\frac{1}{2} + 2\frac{1}{2} =$

$2\frac{2}{3} + 2\frac{2}{3} =$

$3\frac{2}{6} - 2\frac{3}{6} =$

$4\frac{2}{5} - 1\frac{4}{5} =$

$2\frac{3}{12} - 1\frac{8}{12} =$

$1\frac{6}{8} + 2\frac{7}{8} =$

Upon completion, add these stickers to your path on the map!

You sail with a friend for $2\frac{3}{4}$ hours. Then you swim for $\frac{3}{4}$ hour. How much time in all did you spend swimming and sailing?

hours

Plate Tectonics

Upon completion, add this sticker to your path on the map!

Hot Lava! Read about plate tectonics.

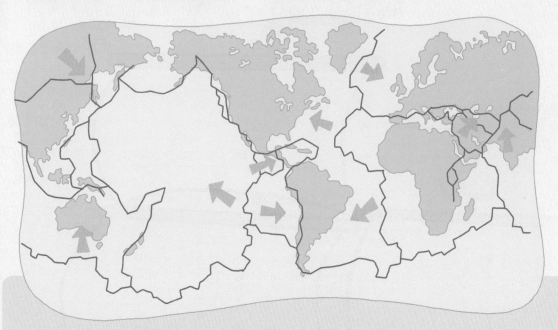

Earth's surface, which is covered by both land and sea, is broken into giant pieces called tectonic plates. They slowly float above Earth's liquid center, moving just a few centimeters each year. It is this movement that creates mountain ranges, earthquakes, volcanoes, and ocean floor structures. Where two plates meet, the following events can occur:

- The plates move alongside each other (in opposite or the same directions), causing earthquakes.

- The plates press against each other, causing earthquakes and the formation of mountains.

- The plates move away from each other, causing earthquakes and volcanoes.

- The plates slip over and under each other, also causing earthquakes and volcanoes.

Study each diagram. Then write what happens as a result: earthquakes, volcanoes, and/or new mountains.

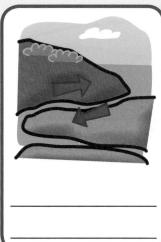

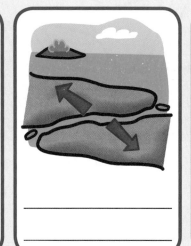

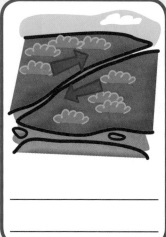

Instant Island

Read about how a volcano forms an island. Then read each
statement and write **T** if it is true or **F** if it is false.

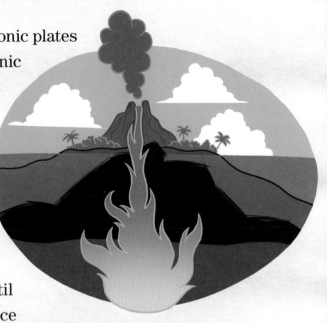

Volcanoes form where two tectonic plates
meet or in the middle of a tectonic
plate because of a hot spot. Hot
spots are especially hot areas
in Earth's mantle. The hot
magma rises up through
the ocean crust. When it
reaches the water, the lava
cools and becomes rock.
Over time, more and more
layers of rock are laid down until
they rise above the ocean surface
to form an island. At first, the island may be warm to the touch! But
eventually, the top layer of rock cools. Meanwhile, the tectonic plate
has slowly moved over the hot spot. The original volcano becomes
inactive. The magma from the hot spot then rises up through a new
part of the oceanic crust, forming a new island close to the first. In
this way, a single hot spot can produce a chain of islands, which is how
scientists believe the Hawaiian Islands formed.

Plate Tectonics

Upon
completion,
add this
sticker to
your path on
the map!

The Hawaiian Islands may have been formed by a single hot spot. _____

A hot spot always flows through the same place in the ocean's crust. _____

Cooled lava forms rock. _____

A hot spot originates in the earth's mantle. _____

All volcanoes form where two tectonic plates meet. _____

Now
add this
sticker
to your
map!

**BONUS: If you saw a shellfish
fossil while on a hike, what
hypothesis might you make
about that area?**

_____

_____

_____

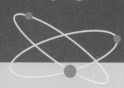

Multiplying
Fractions
and Whole
Numbers

Microscopic Multiplication

Find the products. Multiply the number of plankton by the part that is shaded.

$3 \times \frac{1}{2} =$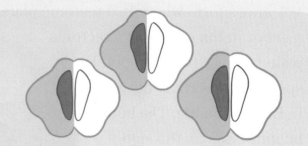

$7 \times \frac{1}{3} =$

$4 \times \frac{5}{6} =$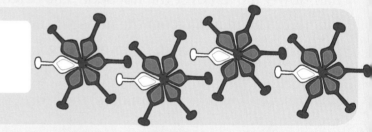

$6 \times \frac{2}{3} =$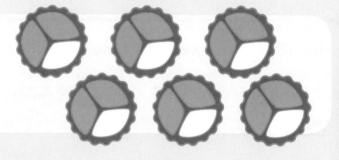

$7 \times \frac{3}{8} =$

$5 \times \dfrac{3}{10} =$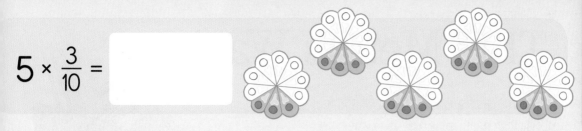

$10 \times \dfrac{2}{4} =$

$3 \times \dfrac{7}{12} =$

Upon
completion,
add these
stickers to
your path on
the map!

$13 \times \dfrac{7}{8} =$

Solve each word problem.

To study plankton in seawater, a biologist collected
14 samples of seawater. Each sample was $\dfrac{2}{3}$ cup.
How many cups of seawater were collected in all?

_____ cups

Biologists collected $\dfrac{3}{4}$ bucket of plankton each day
for 3 days. How many buckets did they collect?

_____ buckets

American Revolution

Upon completion, add this sticker to your path on the map!

Brain Box

The **American Revolution**, 1775 to 1783, was fought to gain independence from Britain. The American colonies listed their reasons for seeking freedom in the **Declaration of Independence** in 1776.

This Means War!

Match each excerpt from the Declaration of Independence to a simplified explanation.

He (the King of Great Britain) has refused his assent to laws, the most wholesome and necessary for the public good.

The King won't allow necessary laws to be passed in the colonies.

He has kept among us, in times of peace, Standing Armies without the Consent of our legislatures.

Colonists are being punished for alleged crimes without ever being given a jury trial.

For Quartering large bodies of armed troops among us.

The King has sent his army to patrol the colonies, against their will, though it is not wartime.

For protecting them [soldiers], by a mock Trial, from punishment for any Murders which they should commit on the Inhabitants of these States.

The King allows his troops to live in the homes of colonists without their permission.

For depriving us in many cases, of the benefits of Trial by Jury.

When soldiers are accused of murdering colonists, they are put on trial, but it is only for show; the soldiers are always declared innocent.

BONUS: Put the following grievance into your own words: For cutting off our Trade with all parts of the world.

Now add this sticker to your map!

Hire Me!

Read the chart. Then use the transitional words and phrases in the first column to fill in the blanks. (HINT: Some words can be used interchangeably.)

Transitional Words and Phrases

Upon completion, add this sticker to your path on the map!

If You Say:	You Mean:
Also, In addition, Moreover	This thought will **add** to my previous thought.
Although, Yet, On the other hand	This thought will **contrast** my previous thought.
For example, For instance	This thought will **illustrate** my previous thought
In other words, Specifically	This thought will **clarify** my previous thought

Dear Ms. Shelly Delray:

Please consider me for the open position at Shelly's Snack Shack. I have good people skills, and I love talking to people. I _____ love to cook and have experience making sandwiches and snacks. _____ I have never worked at a snack bar, I baby-sat all last summer and made breakfast and lunch for the kids every day. I did this in a very hectic environment. _____, I once had to make five peanut butter sandwiches while breaking up a fight between twin toddlers. _____, I am well prepared for even the busiest of days at Shelly's Snack Shack. I can start May 25.

Thank you,

Matthew Craig

Salt Marsh Math

Write the fraction of the box that has critters.
Then write the decimal equivalent.

Fraction and Decimal Equivalents

Upon completion, add this sticker to your path on the map!

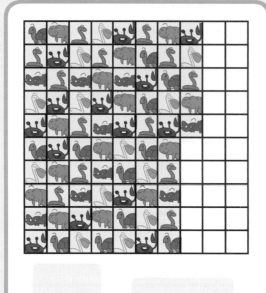

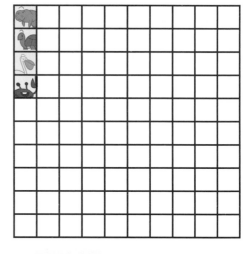

_____ = _____

_____ = _____

Write each fraction as a decimal.

$\frac{29}{100}$ = _____ $\frac{46}{100}$ = _____ $\frac{87}{100}$ = _____

$\frac{3}{100}$ = _____ $\frac{30}{100}$ = _____ $\frac{98}{100}$ = _____

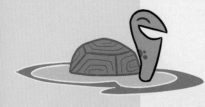

Write each decimal as a fraction.

0.02 = _____   0.45 = _____   0.6 = _____

Brain Box

If there are fewer than 10 hundredths in a decimal, you write a 0 in the tenths column.

Example: **0.01** = $\frac{1}{100}$

tenths   hundredths

Level 5A complete!

Add this achievement sticker
to your path...

...and move on to

Level 6A
on page 96!

...OR GO ON AN
OUTSIDE QUEST
AND MOVE ON
TO LEVEL 6B
ON PAGE 112!

Amazing Animals!

Use your own words to rewrite each
incomplete sentence or run-on sentence.

Complete
Sentences

START
LEVEL
5B
HERE!

Upon
completion,
add this
sticker to
your path on
the map!

Big Major Cay is an uninhabited island
somehow it has feral pigs living on it
and swimming in its waters!

_____

_____

If you ever go to the pigs' island.

_____

_____

Orcas have many distinct ways of life, such as some hunt large
marine mammals others mainly eat small fish.

_____

_____

Since rats are good swimmers.

_____

_____

If sharks can smell a drop of blood in a million drops of water.

_____

_____

Brain Box

A dependent clause needs an independent clause; otherwise, it is an **incomplete sentence**.
   Incomplete sentence example: When an orca leapt.
   Complete sentence example: When an orca leapt, the fisherman yelped.

Two or more independent clauses without a comma and conjunction make a **run-on sentence**.
   Run-on sentence example: Whales dive deep then they must come up for air.
   Compound sentence example: Whales dive deep, but then they must come up for air.

Escape from Alcatraz!

Combine the sentences to form a compound sentence.

Alcatraces means "pelicans" in Spanish. Alcatraz was once a haven for pelicans.

_____

_____

Then it became an island prison. Federal prisoners who had attempted escapes from other prisons were often sent to Alcatraz.

_____

_____

Upon
completion,
add this
sticker to
your path on
the map!

In all, 36 inmates tried to escape. Most were stopped, captured, or later found to have drowned.

_____

_____

Five prisoners were never found. They may have completed the 1.5-mile swim to shore.

_____

_____

Brain Box

Today, the Escape from Alcatraz Triathlon begins with the same 1.5-mile swim. Participants are encouraged to wear protective wet suits.

_____

_____

Simple or short
sentences can
be **combined**
with a **comma**
and a
conjunction,
(and, but, for,
nor, or, so, yet,
because) to
make a
compound
sentence.

84

Scientific Method

Rock It, Scientist!

Read about Jax's experiment. Then fill in his lab report.

Jax wondered if an orange could float with or without its peel. He guessed that it could only float without the peel because it would be lighter. He found two oranges that were the same size. Then he peeled one orange and left the other unpeeled. He filled two bowls with the same amount of water each. He dropped an orange into each bowl. To his surprise, the unpeeled orange floated and the peeled orange did not!

Upon completion, add this sticker to your path on the map!

The question: _____

_____

The hypothesis: _____

_____

_____

Description of the experiment: _____

_____

Results and observations: _____

_____

Conclusion (Was the hypothesis correct?): _____

_____

BONUS: If, for the past 10 years, summers in Boston had been warmer, and more jellyfish had been seen in the bay, what is one hypothesis that you might make from this information?

_____

_____

Now add this sticker to your map!

Summer Brain Quest: Between Grades 4 &

Underwater Angles

Draw each geometric figure. Then use each figure to draw an underwater object or animal.

Geometric Figures

Upon completion, add this sticker to your path on the map!

A point

A line

Parallel lines

Perpendicular lines

Two different angles

Brain Box

A **point** in space

A **line** goes on forever in both directions.

Parallel lines are lines that are the same distance apart at every point and never meet or cross.

Perpendicular lines are lines that cross to make a right angle (90°, or a square corner).

When lines meet at a point, they form an angle.

Research

I've Always Wondered . . .

Choose a topic to research or write in your own topic. Then find two sources on your chosen topic and cite them as shown below. Lastly, read about your topic in your sources.

TOPICS

Jellyfish

The *Titanic*

Ring of Fire (in the Pacific)

Surfing

My topic: _____

_____

BIBLIOGRAPHY

My First Source

_____

_____

_____

_____

My Second Source

_____

_____

_____

_____

Brain Box

To research a topic for **informative writing**, read several **reliable sources**. Reliable sources include books by reputable writers, unbiased newspapers and magazines, and websites of museums and universities. Cite sources in a **bibliography** as follows:

Book
Author Last Name, Author First Name. *Name of Book*. City of Publication: Publisher, Date.

Article
Author Last Name, Author First Name. "Name of Article." *Name of the Publication*. Date.

Website
Author Last Name, Author First Name. "Title of Article." Name of website. Date (if provided). Website URL.

Paraphrasing is putting an author's words and ideas into your own words and crediting the original source. That way, you show that you understand what you are reading, and you also avoid **plagiarizing** (copying another author's words or ideas and not crediting the author).

Noted

On the opposite page, circle one of the sources that you read. Paraphrase three facts from the source.

Research

FACT #1

FACT #2

FACT #3

Upon completion, add these stickers to your path on the map!

The
Constitution

Law of the Land

Read about the different parts of the Constitution.

The **preamble** states the purpose of the constitution.

We the People of the United States, in Order to form a more perfect Union, establish Justice, insure domestic Tranquility . . .

The seven original **articles** state how the government will work. They describe the powers held by legislative, executive, and judicial branches; state rights and responsibilities; and the process of making constitutional amendments. They also state that the Constitution is the supreme law of the land.

All legislative Powers herein granted shall be vested in a Congress of the United States, which shall consist of a Senate and House of Representatives.

Brain Box

Created in 1787 and ratified in 1788, the **U.S. Constitution** is the set of laws that governs the United States as a nation. It describes the system of federal government and state and individual rights.

The 27 **amendments** are laws that were added to the Constitution. The first 10, known as the **Bill of Rights**, protect the basic rights of citizens.

Amendment I: Congress shall make no law respecting an establishment of religion, or prohibiting the free exercise thereof; or abridging the freedom of speech, or of the press; or the right of the people peaceably to assemble, and to petition the Government for a redress of grievances.

You and 200 other kids are shipwrecked on an island. Write a constitution to govern yourselves.

The Constitution

Preamble (State the purpose of your constitution.)

_____

_____

_____

Articles (State how your government will work.)

_____

_____

_____

_____

_____

Bill of Rights (State three basic rights that all citizens will have.)

_____

_____

_____

_____

_____

Upon completion, add these stickers to your path on the map!

BONUS: A submarine with twenty newcomers docks on your island. What rights do these visitors have or not have on your island?

_____

_____

_____

_____

Now add this sticker to your map!

Prepositional Phrases

In the Southern Ocean

Underline the prepositional phrase or phrases in each sentence.

The skua seabird flies menacingly over the penguins.

The penguins dive under the iceberg.

The iceberg floats alongside our ship.

The ship sails beside a family of whales.

During high tide, a whale becomes stranded on the beach.

We work through the night to save the whale.

As night turns into day, we launch the creature into the bay.

Beyond the bay, the whale's pod waits for it.

Upon completion, add this sticker to your path on the map!

Write a sentence that contains one or more prepositional phrases.

Brain Box

A **preposition** shows how nouns relate to other words in a sentence. A preposition often shows **where** something is or **when** something happened.

Example: We canoed **through the fjord**. Where? **Through the fjord.**

Together, a preposition and noun make up a **prepositional phrase.** Any words used to describe the noun are also part of the phrase.

Example: She dove **into the murky lagoon.**

Haunted Beach House

Read the story. Underline inappropriate shifts in verb tense. Then write the correct verb tense below.

Verb Tense

Upon completion, add this sticker to your path on the map!

Last summer, my mom rented a beach house for the whole summer. I was so excited! But when we get there, it is an abandoned shack. The windows were broken, the weeds were overgrown, and sand was everywhere.

My mom called the owner to complain, but no one answered. She asked a neighbor if there was another number where we could reach him. The neighbor says the owner has been dead for five years. Then how was my mom able to talk to him in the first place? Gulp!

Since we couldn't figure out how to get our money back, we decide to clean the house and fix the windows. It took all week! While my mom and I were cleaning the yard, a girl my age rode her bike past us. I waved hello, but she didn't wave back.

"Who are you waving to?" my mom asks.

"That girl riding her bike in the street," I say.

"Abi," my mom said. "There is no girl in the street."

A chill went down my back. What was going on here? And do I have the courage to find out?

Brain Box

A story can have both **past** and **present** tenses, but there must be a reason for the shift.

Example: "I live in Chicago. My family moved here last June." The tense shifts because the narrator currently lives in Chicago, but he or she moved there in the past.

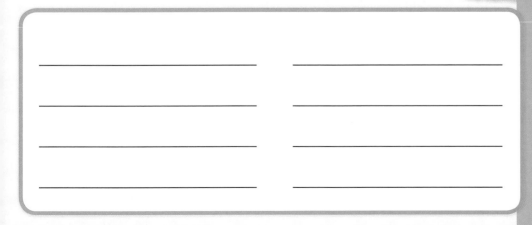

Fight for Your Rights!

The United States of Mermaids has the same Bill of Rights as we do. Some of the amendments are listed below. Read them, and then write which right has been violated in each scenario.

AMENDMENT I
The right to freedom of religion, freedom of speech, freedom of the press, and freedom to peaceably assemble

AMENDMENT II
The freedom to bear arms as part of a well-regulated militia

AMENDMENT III
The right not to be required to house soldiers

AMENDMENT IV
The right not to be searched or to have your home or belongings searched without a warrant

AMENDMENT V
The right to due process, which includes a grand jury for a capital crime, not having to testify against oneself, and the right not to be tried twice for the same crime

AMENDMENT VI
The right to a speedy and fair trial, including the right to have an attorney and an impartial jury

Aqualina is on trial for stealing a precious pearl. One of the jurors is friends with the prosecutor.

_____

Shelly was arrested for writing an article that criticized President Ursula's oppressive policies.

_____

While Coral was out, police searched the wrecked ship in which she'd been living.

_____

Upon completion, add this sticker to your path on the map!

Brain Box

The first 10 amendments to the **U.S. Constitution** are collectively called the **Bill of Rights**. It grants basic rights to all Americans . . . and, perhaps, mermaids.

Open Wide

Use the protractor to estimate the angle measure of the fish's mouth to the nearest 10° (degrees).

about _____°

about _____°

about _____°

about _____°

Measuring Angles

Upon completion, add this sticker to your path on the map!

BONUS: Is the puffer fish's smile at an angle greater than 90°? Compare it with a fish from above and explain why or why not.

Now add this sticker to your map!

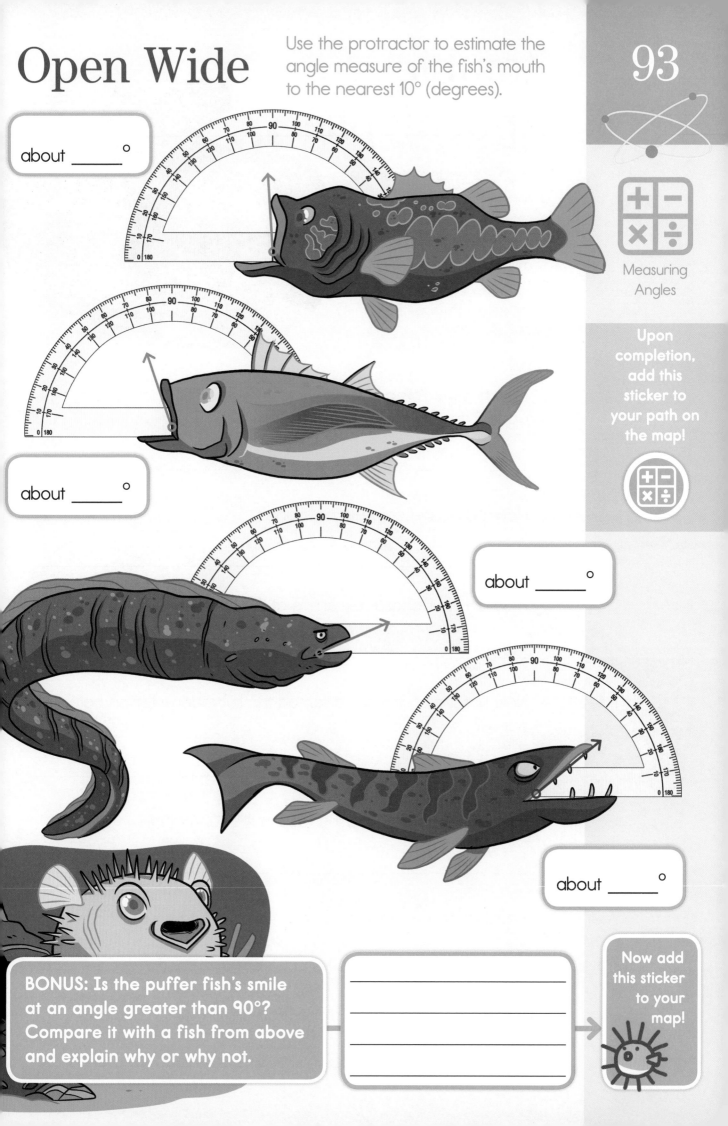

Characters

Brain Box

Zombie Apocalypse

Imagine a character living alone in an abandoned submarine during a zombie apocalypse. (And the zombies can swim.) Describe your character. Answer each question and be as specific as possible.

How has the zombie apocalypse affected the character's appearance (is he/she injured, dirty, etc.)?

_____

How did he/she come to be alone?

_____

How did your character arrive at the submarine?

_____

How has the character adapted the submarine for his/her needs?

_____

What dangers does he/she face in the submarine?

_____

How has he/she been surviving?

_____

What does he/she want more than anything in the world?

_____

Level 5B complete!

Add this achievement sticker
to your path...

... AND GO ON
AN OUTSIDE QUEST
AND MOVE ON
TO LEVEL 6A
ON PAGE 96!

... or move on to
Level 6B
on page 112!

Surf's Up!

Label each angle as acute, right, or obtuse.

START
LEVEL
6A
HERE!

Angles

Brain Box

An **angle** is formed where two line segments meet.

A **right angle** is 90°.

An **acute angle** is less than 90°.

An **obtuse angle** is greater than 90°.

Color Your Ride

Angles

Upon completion, add these stickers to your path on the map!

Color the acute triangles **blue**.
Color the right triangles **red**.
Color the obtuse triangles **yellow**.

Brain Box

Every triangle has three angles.

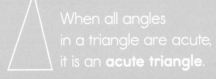

When a triangle has one right angle, it is a **right triangle**.

When all angles in a triangle are acute, it is an **acute triangle**.

When a triangle has one obtuse angle, it is an **obtuse triangle**.

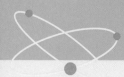

Information Writing

The Naked Truth

Use the facts about naked mole rats to write a paragraph in your own words. Include an introductory sentence, three supporting sentences, and a concluding sentence. Also use linking words and phrases.

Naked mole rats are rodents.

They live in clans of 20 to 300, which are similar to ant colonies or beehives.

There is one queen, which is the only clan member to bear children.

There are workers, which are responsible for digging the burrows, gathering roots to eat, and taking care of the queen and her babies.

There are also soldiers, which sound the alarm if a predator enters the burrows and will gather together to chase the enemy away.

Females fight for the position of queen, and the queen may be overthrown at any time.

The burrows have rooms, including a nursery, where the queen cares for her babies; a pantry for storing food; and even a bathroom.

Upon completion, add this sticker to your path on the map!

Upsides and Downsides

Read about the Industrial Revolution. Underline the positive outcomes and circle the negative outcomes. Draw a line through the neutral outcomes.

The Industrial Revolution led to a new way of life for everyone. In preindustrial America, small farms provided a living for many families. During the Industrial Revolution, farming practices and machines became more efficient, leading to greater food production. More abundant food led to better health, which in turn lowered the death rate and raised the birth rate.

Meanwhile, with the invention of water-powered machines, large factories replaced the small shops in which workers once built products from start to finish. The factories provided jobs to the nation's growing population. Unfortunately, the workers endured long hours for low pay under dangerous conditions. Moreover, as towns and cities grew up around the factories, overcrowding became an issue and diseases became rampant.

Anxious to stop the suffering, doctors researched the causes of the diseases, and learned that many spread through dirty water. Armed with this knowledge, cities created sanitary sewage systems. Other changes in living conditions were slower to come about, and sickness was still a problem. However, the improved technology of the Industrial Revolution had set in motion advances that would lead to better health care and a higher quality of life in the industrial world. Unfortunately, it also introduced a new public health concern: the air pollution caused by burning fossil fuels, such as coal, oil, and natural gas, to produce electricity and power factories.

Brain Box

The **Industrial Revolution** swept across England from 1760 to 1850, and by around 1850, had a firm foothold in America. It was a time marked by innovations in agriculture and manufacturing, and a shift from agricultural life to city living for many people.

Hot or Cold?

Read about the climate clues. Then look at the pictures to determine whether they indicate a hot or cold climate in the past. Circle the blue thermometer for cold or the red thermometer for hot.

> Glacial till is a mixture of sand, clay, gravel, and rock deposited by glaciers as they flowed over land.

> Red rocks are colored red from iron deposits that occur in a hot desert.

> Corals are communities of animals that live in tropical, or warm, ocean water. Over time, corals form a structure called a coral reef.

> Rock striations are long scratches in bedrock caused by debris in glaciers scraping the ground as the glaciers flow over the landscape.

Brain Box

Climate is the weather in a given place over time. Scientists read clues in the landscape, rocks, and fossils to determine how climate has changed through the ages.

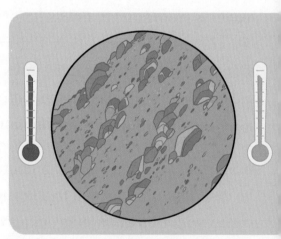

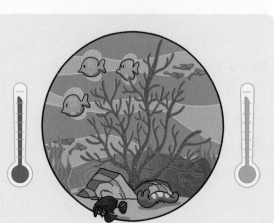

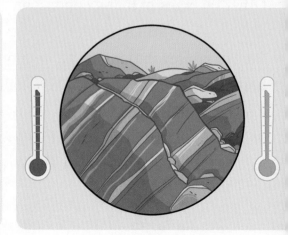

Fossils

Is each fossil symmetrical? If so, draw a line of symmetry.

Draw all of the lines of symmetry. Write how many lines of symmetry each shape has.

Brain Box

A shape has a **line of symmetry** if it can be folded along the line so that the two parts match exactly.

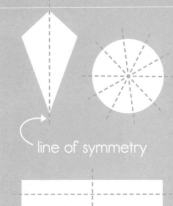

line of symmetry

Adaptation

I'm a Survivor!

Read the passages describing cactus and conifer adaptations.

When it rains, the cactus sprouts more **roots**. These shallow roots quickly absorb water and transport it to the stem.

The **stem** stores water, which can be used in times of drought. A waxy coating results in less water evaporating from the stem. The spines covering the stem protect it from thirsty animals that would bite into it for a drink.

The **spines** are actually adapted leaves. Their narrow structure means that less water is lost through transpiration. The spines do not perform photosynthesis; the stem does this job instead. That's why it's green!

Though a cactus stem repels animals, its **flowers** attract them with colors and scents. The animals pollinate the flowers, resulting in berries—the **seeds** that grow into new cacti.

The cone **shape** of the evergreen allows heavy snow to slide off the tree, so that branches don't break.

The **needles** are adapted leaves that can store water throughout the year. Their narrow structure and waxy coating prevent water loss through transpiration. The smaller surface area of the leaves would seem to make photosynthesis less efficient. However, this is made up for by the sheer number of needles. The needles are not shed annually, but only every few years. This conserves energy, which is important in cold climates, where sunlight is sparse in wintertime. Finally, needles also taste bad, warding off hungry animals.

Conifers do not have **flowers** to attract animals and insects. Instead, male and female **pinecones** reproduce through wind pollination. The **seeds** grow in the pinecone.

Adaptation

Fill in the chart by writing a checkmark (✓) in each category that applies.

	Cactus	Evergreen
Narrow, adapted leaves result in reduced water loss.		
Adapted leaves have features that repel animals.		
Leaves are shed each fall.		
Photosynthesis occurs in the stem rather than in the leaves.		
A waxy coating on the plant prevents water loss.		
The plant has a cone shape.		
The stem stores water.		
Flowers attract animals for pollination.		
Pollination occurs through wind only.		

Upon completion, add these stickers to your path on the map!

CONGRATULATIONS!
You completed all of the science quests in this path! You earned:

Write and Evaluate Expressions

Messages in a Bottle

Write the numerical expression. Then find the value.

Add 3 and 7, then subtract 5.

Multiply 5 and 2, then add 7.

Multiply 5 by the sum of 2 and 7.

Add 4 and 6, then multiply by 2.

Divide 25 by 5, then add 6.

Divide 20 by 10 minus 5.

Subtract the quotient of 12 divided by 2 from 20.

Add the product of 3 times 6 and the product of 4 times 2.

Subtract 50 from 10 times 6.

Brain Box

When evaluating expressions, follow the **order of operations**.
Complete operations in parentheses first. Then multiply and divide in order from left to right. Then add and subtract in order from left to right.

(3 + 5) x 3 = 24   Add 3 and 5, then multiply by 3.   Parentheses are needed.

3 x 3 + 4 = 13   Multiply 3 and 3, then add 4.   No parentheses needed.

36 ÷ (2 + 4) = 6   Divide 36 by the sum of 2 and 4.   Parentheses needed.

49 ÷ 7 + 7 = 14   Divide 49 by 7, then add 7.   No parentheses needed.

Driftwood Matches

Draw a line to match each expression with the answer.

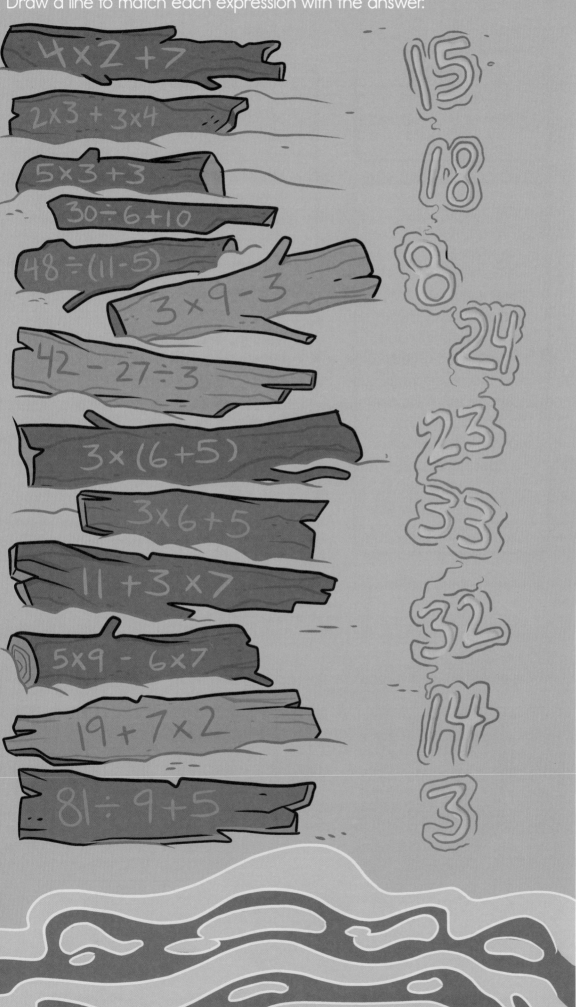

$4 \times 2 + 7$

$2 \times 3 + 3 \times 4$

$5 \times 3 + 3$

$30 \div 6 + 10$

$48 \div (11 - 5)$

$3 \times 9 - 3$

$42 - 27 \div 3$

$3 \times (6 + 5)$

$3 \times 6 + 5$

$11 + 3 \times 7$

$5 \times 9 - 6 \times 7$

$19 + 7 \times 2$

$81 \div 9 + 5$

15

18

8

24

23

33

32

14

3

Write and Evaluate Expressions

Upon completion, add these stickers to your path on the map!

Westward Expansion

Upon completion, add this sticker to your path on the map!

Explore!

Read the timeline. Then write the date that Lewis and Clark reached each point on the map.

May 14, 1804
Lewis and Clark depart St. Louis via the Missouri River.

November 4, 1804
Lewis and Clark hire Sacagawea (a Shoshone) and her husband as interpreters near present-day Bismarck, North Dakota. Sacagawea, the only woman on the Corps of Discovery Expedition, was helpful in many ways, such as reading the landscape.

August 12, 1805
Lewis finds the headwaters of the Missouri River in present-day Montana, but learns that there is no easy water route to the Pacific Ocean. The Corps is now in Shoshone territory, and Sacagawea reunites with her brother, who trades horses and mules with the group, so that they can cross the mountains.

September 23, 1805
Nearly starving after their mountain journey, the Corps is rescued by the Nez Perce Indians in present-day Idaho.

November 24, 1805
The Corps of Discovery reaches the Pacific Ocean—mission accomplished!

Brain Box

After the **Louisiana Purchase** in 1803, President Thomas Jefferson employed Meriwether Lewis to explore the area and gather information about the people, plants, animals, and weather while en route to the Pacific Ocean. Lewis chose his friend William Clark to be his co-commander; the larger group of explorers was known as the **Corps of Discovery**.

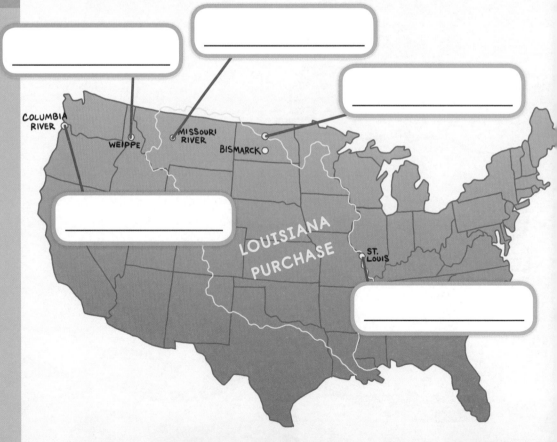

Digging into Dialogue

Write three lines of dialogue for a pair of characters. Use quotation marks and indicate who said what.

"Would you like to come over for lunch?" asked the weasel.

"Ha! That's the oldest line in the book!" said the vole. "I'm supposed to think you're inviting me over to eat lunch, but really, I'm what's on the menu for lunch. You must think I'm really—"

"Delicious," said the weasel.

Dialogue

Upon completion, add this sticker to your path on the map!

_____

_____

_____

_____

_____

Brain Box

Dialogue is a conversation between characters. It can be used to show how they relate to each other. Are they friends? Rivals? What do they want from each other?

BONUS: Put the following quote into your own words. "Use what talent you possess: the woods would be very silent if no birds sang except those that sang best."—Henry Van Dyke

_____

_____

Now add this sticker to your map!

CONGRATULATIONS! You completed all of your English language art quests! You earned:

Tunnel Trouble

Write the standard form of the decimal numbers along the tunnel.

Decimals in Standard Form

Upon completion, add this sticker to your path on the map!

Seven tenths ☐

Seven hundredths ☐

Seven thousandths ☐

Thirteen hundredths ☐

Three hundred twelve thousandths ☐

Seven and twelve hundredths ☐

Two and one hundred nine thousandths ☐

$\frac{1}{10} + \frac{4}{100}$ ☐

$\frac{3}{10} + \frac{9}{100}$ ☐

$\frac{3}{10} + \frac{9}{100} + \frac{7}{1000}$ ☐

$2 + \frac{6}{10} + \frac{2}{100} + \frac{1}{1000}$ ☐

Brain Box

One tenth	$\frac{1}{10}$	0.1
One hundredth	$\frac{1}{100}$	0.01
One thousandth	$\frac{1}{1000}$	0.001
One and two hundred thirty-four thousandths	$1 + \frac{2}{10} + \frac{3}{100} + \frac{4}{1000} = 1.234$	

Crabby Comparisons

Write <, =, or > to compare.
Then answer the questions.

1.486 ◯ 1.386   0.880 ◯ 0.808

0.40 ◯ 0.400   7.545 ◯ 7.445

5.612 ◯ 5.016   0.489 ◯ 0.582

0.529 ◯ 0.922   10.02 ◯ 10.020

0.427 ◯ 0.421   0.045 ◯ 0.054

5.05 ◯ 5.052   0.599 ◯ 0.6

Write three decimal numbers greater than 0.975.

_____

Write three decimal numbers less than 0.889.

_____

Write three decimal numbers between 0.218 and 0.222.

_____

Upon completion, add this sticker to your path on the map!

Brain Box

To compare two decimals, line up the decimal points. Begin at the left, and compare the digits in each place. The greater decimal is the one with the greatest digit farthest to the left. If the digits are the same, move one place to the right and compare those digits.

BONUS: One angelfish is 1.025 inches long and another angelfish is 1.205 inches long. Write two statements using < and > to compare their length.

_____
_____
_____
_____

Now add this sticker to your map!

Puffed-Up Patterns

Write how many times bigger each puffer fish can blow up to.

 ×  = 50

 × [ ] = 600

 × [ ] = 7,000

 × [ ] = 120

 × [ ] = 2,400

 × [ ] = 25,000

 × [ ] = 1,200

Brain Box

To multiply with multiples of ten, first multiply using the basic factor.

Then count the number of zeros in both factors.

$30 \times 70 = ?$

$3 \times 7 = 21$

30×70, two zeros

$30 \times 70 = 2100$

Last, write the product followed by the number of zeros in both factors.

Quest complete!

Add this achievement
sticker to your path…

QUEST
complete!
Welcome to
5th grade!

…and turn to page 128
for your Summer Brainiac
Award!

Remember When...

Complete each sentence to brainstorm ideas for a true story about your life.

Everything changed the day _____

_____

I learned a lot when _____

_____

When I was younger, I made the mistake of _____

_____

A memory I have about being around water is _____

_____

I'll never forget the summer vacation when _____

_____

One of the hardest things I've ever had to do is _____

_____

I can't believe I was brave enough to _____

_____

Brain Box

A **narrative** is a true or imagined story. It should have a **theme**, a **point of view**, and **vivid descriptions**.

Circle one of the sentences from page 112. Rewrite it at the top of this page. Then finish the story, including vivid details, your thoughts about what happened, and a statement about what this experience taught you.

Narrative
Writing

Upon
completion,
add these
stickers to
your path on
the map!

_____

_____

_____

_____

_____

_____

_____

_____

_____

_____

_____

_____

_____

_____

_____

_____

Cuckoo for Coconuts

Read about the parts of a coconut palm. Then label the diagram with the words in the box.

Plants

Upon completion, add this sticker to your path on the map!

Though palm roots are short, they are plentiful and work together to soak up water and nutrients and to anchor the tree to the ground. The stem (sometimes called a trunk) transports water and nutrients from the roots to the leaves in a system of pipes called the vascular system. Through photosynthesis, the green leaves transform water, sunlight, and nutrients into carbohydrates: the plant's food. Under the leaves, male and female flowers reproduce through pollination by insects and wind. They produce a buoyant fruit: the coconut! Inside the fruit is a single large seed. From this seed a new coconut palm grows. The part of the coconut that people eat is called the endosperm. It nourishes the newly sprouted seed.

roots	fruit
stem	seed
leaves	flower
endosperm	

BONUS: Coconut palms grow wild in warm coastal areas throughout the world. How might the seeds (coconuts) have dispersed to all the continents?

Now add this sticker to your map!

Shell We Dance?

Answer each question.

An expert says there are about 85,000 different varieties of mollusks (animals with seashells). Explain how 84,637 could be the actual number rounded. (To what place is it rounded?)

Rounding and Estimating Answers

_____

_____

A clamshell in a museum is roughly 140 centimeters wide. If that number is rounded to the nearest ten, what is the largest and the smallest number the exact measurements could be?

_____

_____

There are 22 similar display cases of shells. If one display case has 97 shells, use rounding to estimate the number of shells displayed in that room. Explain how you found your answer.

_____

_____

A museum estimates it has 220,000 different shells. If 215,754 is the exact number, explain how rounding results in that estimate.

_____

_____

Suppose you find 12 shells a day for 15 days. Estimate the total number of shells you will collect. Explain two ways you could round to find your answer. Which way do you think is more accurate? Why?

_____

_____

Poetry

The Absolute Worst

Read the excerpt of this poem by Lewis Carroll.
Then answer each question.

A Sea Dirge

by Lewis Carroll

There are certain things—as, a spider, a ghost,
The income-tax, gout, an umbrella for three—
That I hate, but the thing that I hate the most
Is a thing they call the Sea. . . .

. . . It is pleasant and dreamy, no doubt, to float
With 'thoughts as boundless, and souls as free':
But, suppose you are very unwell in the boat,
How do you like the Sea? . . .

. . . If you like your coffee with sand for dregs,
A decided hint of salt in your tea,
And a fishy taste in the very eggs—
By all means choose the Sea.

And if, with these dainties to drink and eat,
You prefer not a vestige of grass or tree,
And a chronic state of wet in your feet,
Then—I recommend the Sea.

For I have friends who dwell by the coast—
Pleasant friends they are to me!
It is when I am with them I wonder most
That anyone likes the Sea. . . .

Brain Box

Stanzas, **meter**, and **rhyme** provide the structure of poems. A stanza consists of lines grouped together in the poem. Meter is the rhythm of the poem, or the number of syllables per line and the pattern in which syllables are stressed. Rhyme is the repetition of the ending sounds of words.

Name three complaints the narrator has about the sea.

_____

_____

_____

Underline the stanza in which the narrator describes how the sea affects food and drink.

Circle the correct rhyme pattern in each stanza.

Lines 1 and 4 rhyme, and lines 2 and 3 rhyme.

Lines 1 and 3 only rhyme.

Lines 1 and 3 rhyme, and lines 2 and 4 rhyme.

Using the Venn diagram, brainstorm things you don't like, things that lots of people like, and things that lots of people like but you do not. Write each in the correct space.

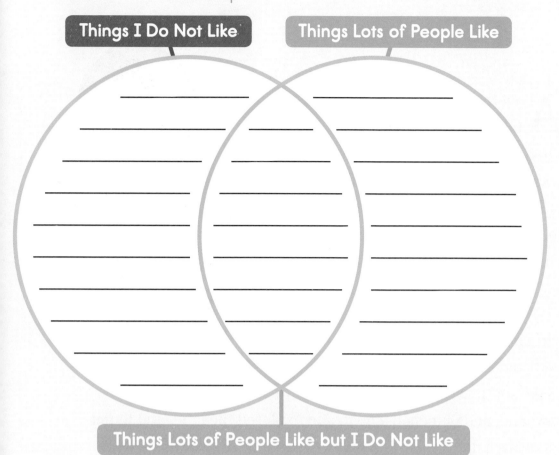

Things I Do Not Like

Things Lots of People Like

Things Lots of People Like but I Do Not Like

Poetry

Upon completion, add these stickers to your path on the map!

Choose one item from the Venn diagram above. Write a poem with a rhyme scheme where lines 1 and 3 rhyme, and lines 2 and 4 rhyme. Fill in the blanks for the first stanza. Then write one more stanza.

There are certain things, as _____ , _____ ,
_____ , _____ , and _____
That I hate, but the thing that I hate the most
Is a thing they call _____
_____
_____
_____
_____

Now add this sticker to your map!

BONUS: Imagine that you are a dinosaur. Write a rhyming stanza about something that you love.

_____
_____
_____
_____

Age of
Exploration

Erik the Red

Read the passage from the *Saga of Erik the Red*.
Then answer the questions.

About this time there began to be much talk at Brattahlid to the effect that Vinland the Good should be explored, for, it was said, that country must be possessed of many goodly qualities. And so it came to pass, that Karlsefni and Snorri fitted out their ship, for the purpose of going in search of that country in the spring . . .

They had in all one hundred and sixty men, when they sailed to the Western Settlement, and thence to Bjarney (Bear Island). They bore away to the southward two *doegr* (12-hour time periods). Then they saw land, and launched a boat, and explored the land, and found there large flat stones, and many of these were twelve ells wide (twelve feet wide—one ell equals 45 inches). There were many Arctic foxes there. They gave a name to the country, and called it Helluland (Land of Flat Stones). Then they sailed with northerly winds two *doegr*, and land then lay before them, and upon it was a great wood and many wild beasts; an island lay off the land to the southeast, and there they found a bear, and they called this Bjarney, while the land where the wood was they called Markland (Forest-land). Thence they sailed southward along the land for a long time, and came to a cape . . .

Brain Box

The **Saga of Erik the Red** describes the Viking exploration of North America around 1000 CE. It was written in the thirteenth century based on oral history. Vinland is thought to be modern-day Newfoundland—this means that the Vikings reached America nearly 500 years before Columbus.

What key detail from the text indicates that the land described must have had an Arctic climate?

_____

_____

Many historians believe Vinland refers to modern-day Newfoundland. Name evidence from the text that could be used to determine the location of Vinland.

_____

_____

The men on board planned to start a settlement in Vinland. Name ten items that you would bring with you to a new land to ensure that you had adequate food and shelter.

_____

_____

_____

_____

_____

_____

_____

_____

_____

What would you name your settlement, and why?

_____

_____

_____

_____

Age of Exploration

Upon completion, add these stickers to your path on the map!

CONGRATULATIONS! You completed all of the social studies quests in this path! You earned:

Water Cycle

Rain Is a Good Thing

Read the definitions related to the water cycle. Then label the diagram with the bold name for each process.

Evaporation: the process of water changing into vapor (gas) as it warms

Transpiration: the process of plants absorbing water at their roots and then releasing water vapor into the atmosphere through their leaves

Condensation: the process of water vapor changing to water droplets (liquid); this is how clouds form.

Precipitation: water falling to the ground as rain, snow, or ice

Surface runoff: water from precipitation that flows over land and seeps into the groundwater or makes its way into lakes, streams, and oceans

Upon completion, add this sticker to your path on the map!

BONUS: Brainstorm 3 ways that you could conserve water at home, school, or other places you go.

_____

_____

_____

Now add this sticker to your map!

Water, Water Everywhere?

Read about the earth's water and study the pie chart. Then fill in the chart.

Water Cycle

Because 75 percent of Earth is covered by water, it may seem like an abundant resource. However, we currently use only freshwater, not salt water, for drinking, cooking, and irrigating fields. Moreover, much of our freshwater is unusable because it is frozen in glaciers or polluted.

Where Earth's Water Is Stored

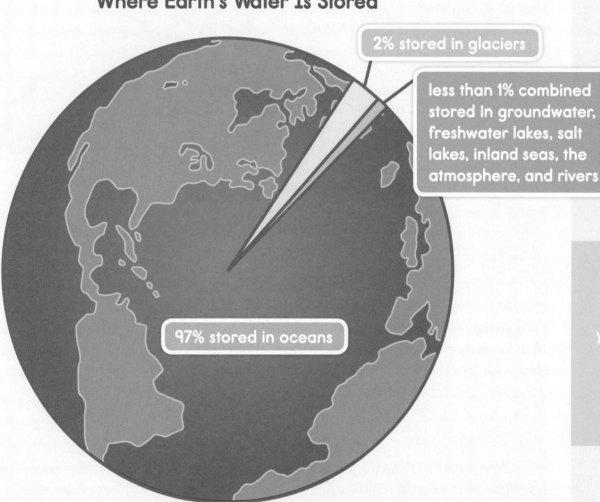

2% stored in glaciers

less than 1% combined stored in groundwater, freshwater lakes, salt lakes, inland seas, the atmosphere, and rivers

97% stored in oceans

Upon completion, add this sticker to your path on the map!

Body of Water	Percentage of the World's Water
Ocean	
Glacier	
Groundwater, freshwater lakes, saltwater lakes, inland seas, the atmosphere, and rivers	

The Little Mermaid

Read the excerpt from "The Little Mermaid" by Hans Christian Andersen. Then answer the questions.

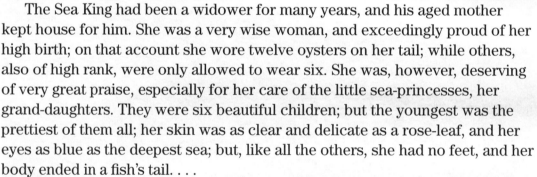

Far out in the ocean, where the water is as blue as the prettiest cornflower, and as clear as crystal, it is very, very deep; so deep, indeed, that no cable could fathom it: many church steeples, piled one upon another, would not reach from the ground beneath to the surface of the water above. There dwell the Sea King and his subjects. . . .

In the deepest spot of all, stands the castle of the Sea King. Its walls are built of coral, and the long, gothic windows are of the clearest amber. The roof is formed of shells that open and close as the water flows over them. Their appearance is very beautiful, for in each lies a glittering pearl, which would be fit for the diadem of a queen.

The Sea King had been a widower for many years, and his aged mother kept house for him. She was a very wise woman, and exceedingly proud of her high birth; on that account she wore twelve oysters on her tail; while others, also of high rank, were only allowed to wear six. She was, however, deserving of very great praise, especially for her care of the little sea-princesses, her grand-daughters. They were six beautiful children; but the youngest was the prettiest of them all; her skin was as clear and delicate as a rose-leaf, and her eyes as blue as the deepest sea; but, like all the others, she had no feet, and her body ended in a fish's tail. . . .

She was a strange child, quiet and thoughtful; and while her sisters would be delighted with the wonderful things which they obtained from the wrecks of vessels, she cared for nothing but her pretty red flowers, like the sun, excepting a beautiful marble statue. It was the representation of a handsome boy, carved out of pure white stone, which had fallen to the bottom of the sea from a wreck. She planted by the statue a rose-colored weeping willow. It grew splendidly, and very soon hung its fresh branches over the statue, almost down to the blue sands. The shadow had a violet tint, and waved to and fro like the branches; it seemed as if the crown of the tree and the root were at play, and trying to kiss each other.

Nothing gave her so much pleasure as to hear about the world above the sea. She made her old grandmother tell her all she knew of the ships and of the towns, the people and the animals. To her it seemed most wonderful and beautiful to hear that the flowers of the land should have fragrance, and not those below the sea; that the trees of the forest should be green; and that the fishes among the trees could sing so sweetly, that it was quite a pleasure to hear them. Her grandmother called the little birds fishes, or she would not have understood her; for she had never seen birds.

Describe the main character in the story.

_____

_____

Describe the castle setting.

_____

What are three things the Little Mermaid thinks are wonderful about life on land?

_____

_____

The Little Mermaid later falls in love with a prince who lives on land. Underline the event that foreshadows this.

> The Little Mermaid's sisters love to find artifacts in shipwrecks.
>
> The Little Mermaid falls in love with a statue of a boy.

Circle which might be the theme of the story.

> With faith and hard work, anything is possible.
>
> Sometimes in yearning for what we don't have, we take for granted the things that we do have.
>
> To whom much is given, much is expected.

Write a letter to a mermaid who has never been on land. Describe something special about life on land to her.

_____

_____

_____

_____

_____

_____

_____

_____

Reading Literature

Upon completion, add these stickers to your path on the map!

Line Plots with Fractions

Upon completion, add this sticker to your path on the map!

Snorkeling

The line plot shows the number of fish a snorkeler saw at various depths. Use the data to answer each word problem.

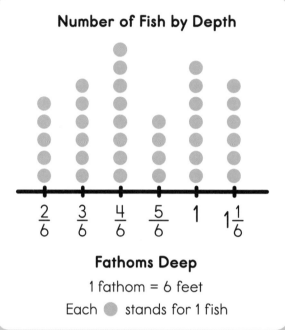

Number of Fish by Depth

$\frac{2}{6}$ $\frac{3}{6}$ $\frac{4}{6}$ $\frac{5}{6}$ 1 $1\frac{1}{6}$

Fathoms Deep

1 fathom = 6 feet

Each ⬤ stands for 1 fish

At how many fathoms deep were the most fish seen?

What is the deepest depth at which fish were seen?

How many fathoms difference is there between the depth where 8 fish were seen and the depth where 5 fish were seen?

How many fathoms difference is there between the deepest and the shallowest places where fish were seen?

A scuba diver can go deeper than a snorkeler. If a diver saw fish at a depth twice as deep as the deepest depth in the line plot above, how many fathoms would that be?

CONGRATULATIONS!
You completed all of the math quests in this path! You earned:

In My Opinion

Imagine that you have sailed around the world and want to share your opinions about what you saw. First, circle one of the four topics below for your opinion piece, and complete the statement if necessary.

Opinion Writing

Upon completion, add this sticker to your path on the map!

Ocean pollution is getting worse. The best way to stop it is _____
_____ .

A student can/can't learn more from real world experiences than from being in school.

_____ **are the smartest animals in the ocean.**

People are happiest living by water.

Next, read a reliable source about your topic. Then write three facts that support your opinion.

_____

_____

_____

_____

Write one or two logical arguments that support your opinion.

_____

_____

_____

_____

Brain Box

An **opinion piece** states a point of view and backs it up with facts and logical arguments. These facts should come from reliable sources.

An **argument** is a reason given to support an opinion or theory. A good argument is truthful and logical.

Write your opinion piece. Start by stating your opinion. Add three to five sentences containing facts or arguments. To link the sentences together, use words like **first**, **second**, **also**, **in addition**, **moreover**, and **however**. Finish with a concluding sentence that summarizes your opinion. Add a title and an illustration.

Opinion Writing

Upon completion, add this sticker to your path on the map!

Quest complete!

Add this achievement sticker to your path...

QUEST complete! Welcome to 5th grade!

...and turn to the next page for your Summer Brainiac Award!

Summer Brainiac Award!

You have completed your entire Summer Brain Quest! Woo-hoo! Congratulations! That's quite an achievement.

Write your name on the line and cut out the award certificate. Show your friends. Hang it on your wall! You're a certified Summer Brainiac!

Summer Brainiac Award

Presented to:

_____

for successfully completing the learning journey in

SUMMER BRAIN QUEST®: BETWEEN GRADES 4&5

Outside Quests

This is not just a workbook—it's a dive into the past, an oceanic adventure, a way to enjoy the summer sunshine, and so much more! Summer is the perfect time to explore the great outdoors. Use the Outside Quests to make your next sunny day more fun than ever—and earn an achievement sticker.

Outside
Quests

Level 1 — Prepositional Hero

Go outside and find features in your environment, such as a sidewalk, a boulder, or a stream. Act out prepositional phrases using the prepositions below. Example: I jumped <u>over the stream</u>. Draw a line through each preposition that you complete.

above   below   over

across   beneath   through

against   beside   toward

alongside   between

around   into

behind   onto

Level 4 — Artifact Inspiration

Find five artifacts (objects made or affected by people) in your neighborhood that might help future archeologists understand life in present-day America. Examples: a street sign, a mural, a tool, a toy, a bike. Then pretend that you are an archeologist who completely misunderstands how each item was used and what each signifies. Prepare a short speech detailing your misguided view on each artifact.

It was used as a calendar.

Level 4A — Water Map

After a rainfall, go outside and draw a map of your neighborhood that includes permanent and temporary bodies of water. Indicate natural features like ponds and creeks, as well as man-made features such as public swimming pools and fountains. Make note of any wildlife you see near the water.

Now add this sticker to your map!

Level 5A — Tell Me 'bout the Good Old Days

Ask an elderly neighbor or relative to tell you about how they spent their summers when they were growing up. Then draw a picture with chalk on the sidewalk of how you imagine the "olden" days.

Now add this sticker to your map!

Outside
Quests

Level 5A — Gotta Bounce!

Perform an experiment outside using a large bouncy ball (such as a basketball) and a smaller one (such as a tennis ball). First, drop each separately. Notice how high they bounce (to your knees, waist, etc.). Next, center the small ball on top of the large ball. Release them at exactly the same time. How high does each ball bounce this time? How is this different from the way they bounced separately? Why do you think there is a difference?

Now add this sticker to your map!

Level 5 — Simple Tool Scavenger Hunt

Find a partner. Go for a walk in your neighborhood and see who can be the first to find examples of all the simple tools: an inclined plane, a lever, pulley, wedge, wheel, and screw.

Now add this sticker to your map!

Outside
Quests

Symmetry Search

Take a walk in a park. Look for natural objects that show line symmetry. Having trouble? Create your own design that has line symmetry using a stick for the line. Put identical (or almost identical) natural objects, such as seeds or acorns, on each side of the line to make a symmetrical design.

Now add this sticker to your map!

Factor Face-Off

Go outdoors and grab some small countable objects, such as stones, leaves, or seeds. Count the number of objects you have. Then determine if you can divide the number by 2 with no remainder. Then split the objects into groups of 2. Were you right? If so, 2 is a factor of that number. Continue guessing and making groups of 3, 4, 5, 6, 7, 8, and 9 to find all the factors.

Now add this sticker to your map!

Answer Key

(For pages not included in this section, answers will vary.)

LEVEL 1

page 10

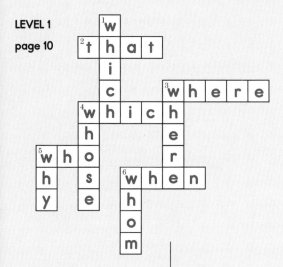

Crossword:
- 1 down: which
- 2 across: that
- 3 across: where
- 4 across: which
- 5 across: who / whose
- why
- 6 across: when / whom

page 11
pirates
the captain of a pirate ship or another pirate
to tell pirates the rules on board the ship
Answers will vary.
Answers will vary.
Answers will vary.

BONUS:
Stone Age tool
cave art
an explorer's diary

page 12
igneous rock
mineral
metamorphic rock

page 13
$20,000 \div 20 = 1,000$
$20,000 = 20 \times 1,000$
$7,000 \div 700 = 10$
$7,000 = 700 \times 10$
$5,000 \div 50 = 100$
$5,000 = 50 \times 100$
$30,000 \div 30 = 1,000$
$30,000 = 30 \times 1,000$

page 14

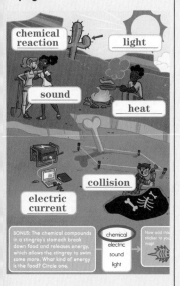

chemical reaction
light
sound
heat
electric current
collision

BONUS: The chemical compounds in a stingray's stomach break down food and releases energy, which allows the stingray to swim some more. What kind of energy is the food? Circle one.

LEVEL 2

page 16

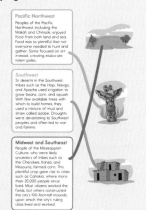

Pacific Northwest
Peoples of the Pacific Northwest, including the Makah and Chinook, enjoyed food from both land and sea. Food was so plentiful that not everyone needed to hunt and gather. Some focused on art instead, creating elaborate totem poles.

Southwest
In deserts in the Southwest, tribes such as the Hopi, Navajo, and Apache used irrigation to grow beans, corn, and squash. With few available trees with which to build homes, they used a mixture of mud and straw called adobe. Droughts were devastating to Southwest peoples and often led to war and famine.

Midwest and Southeast
People of the Mississippian Culture, who were likely ancestors of tribes such as the Cherokee, Kansa, and Missouria, farmed corn. This plentiful crop gave rise to cities such as Cahokia, where more than 20,000 people once lived. Most citizens worked the fields, but others constructed the city's 100-foot-tall mounds, upon which the city's ruling class lived and worked.

page 17
Today I packed a picnic and headed to the beach—barefoot as always. While I was walking, I noticed an eerie stillness. But I brushed it off because, aside from the clouds in the distance, it was a bright, sunny day. So sunny, in fact, that I should have worn flip-flops! I was running to the water to cool my feet when my picnic spilled out of the basket. I grabbed the cookies first, and as I did, a seagull swooped in. I tried to chase it away, but it already was tearing open the sandwich bag. Ugh. Now it was a covered-in-sand-wich. By now, my feet were on fire! I ran to the water, where I promptly dropped the cookies. As I reached for them underwater, I realized I was soaking the chips, too. And that's when I looked up and came face-to-face with a shark. Now it was eyeing ME for a picnic lunch. I dropped everything and swam back to shore. I started over to warn the lifeguard, but realized she was clearing the water already. The clouds had rolled in, and a massive water spout was forming out at sea. It was heading our way! Everyone was running to their cars, and someone plowed right into me. I fell to the ground, thinking, "If I don't hurry, I will be flying through the air in a water spout!" I got myself up and raced home. Now I am sitting in the kitchen, soaked, spooked, and starving. If anyone asks how my day went, I will be telling them that it was no picnic!

BONUS: Answers will vary.

page 18

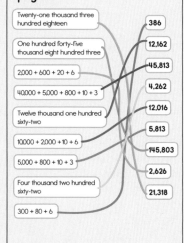

Twenty-one thousand three hundred eighteen — 21,318
One hundred forty-five thousand eight hundred three — 145,803
$2,000 + 600 + 20 + 6$ — 2,626
$40,000 + 5,000 + 800 + 10 + 3$ — 45,813
Twelve thousand one hundred sixty-two — 12,162
$10,000 + 2,000 + 10 + 6$ — 12,016
$5,000 + 800 + 10 + 3$ — 5,813
Four thousand two hundred sixty-two — 4,262
$300 + 80 + 6$ — 386

page 19
$2,287 = 2,000 + 200 + 80 + 7$
$5,256 = 5,000 + 200 + 50 + 6$
$8,543 = 8,000 + 500 + 40 + 3$
$6,911 = 6,000 + 900 + 10 + 1$
$7,943 = 7,000 + 900 + 40 + 3$
$7,921 = 7,000 + 900 + 20 + 1$
$2,28\underline{7} < 5,256 < 6,9\underline{11} < 7,9\underline{21} < 7,94\underline{3} < 8,543$

761,133

BONUS: $700,000 + 60,000 + 1,000 + 100 + 30 + 3$

page 20
a lightweight red surfboard
the crowded city beach
two brave young mermaids
a dangerous white shark
an uninhabited Pacific island

LEVEL 3A

page 24
Ptolemy's
North America and South America
He thought Arabic units were the same as Roman miles, when they were actually much shorter.

page 25
Where are we, Diya?
I don't know, Ryan. But we're alive, and that's the important thing. Now, we need to find fresh water, food, and large stones.
What are the large stones for, Diya?
Well, we need to make an S.O.S. sign. If rescuers fly over us, they'll see it.
Okay, but let's find something to eat first, because I'm starving.
Do you realize we're going to have to fish, hunt, or scavenge for our food?
Why can't we just order something from that tiki hut?
Oh, I guess this isn't a deserted island after all.

page 26
$4 \times 6 = 24$ inches
$18 = 3 \times 6$, 3 times longer
$6 \times 5 = 30$ fish
$6 \times 2 = 12$, 2 times longer

page 27

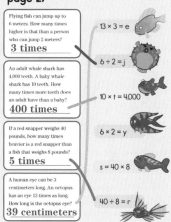

Flying fish can jump up to 6 meters. How many times higher is that than a person who can jump 2 meters? **3 times** — $13 \times 3 = e$

An adult whale shark has 4,000 teeth. A baby whale shark has 10 teeth. How many times more teeth does an adult have than a baby? **400 times** — $6 \div 2 = j$, $10 \times t = 4,000$

If a red snapper weighs 40 pounds, how many times heavier is a red snapper than a fish that weighs 8 pounds? **5 times** — $6 \times 2 = y$, $s = 40 \times 8$

A human eye can be 3 centimeters long. An octopus has an eye 13 times as long. How long is the octopus eye? **39 centimeters** — $40 \div 8 = r$

BONUS: 10 times larger

page 29
Bajau children like to have fun.
Bajau people live, work, and play on the ocean.
Fish provide a healthy diet to the Bajau people.

Answers will vary. **Sample:**

Born to Swim: Life on the Water

Can you imagine learning to swim before you even learned to walk? For the Bajau people of Southeast Asia, that's a way of life. They live and work on boats or in sea homes. As a result, they are great swimmers—even from a young age.

Traditionally, the Bajau have lived in houseboats. Those who still do are so used to life at sea that on land they can feel land sick. Recently, some Bajau have settled in houses on stilts that rise out of the sea. These houses are often connected by wooden boardwalks so that people can walk from house to house. When there is no such boardwalk, people swim to other houses to visit their friends and family.

The Bajau make a living by fishing. They eat the fish and shellfish they catch, and they also trade them for rice and drinking water. The men have a unique way of fishing. They dive up to 66 feet (20 meters) deep. Then they walk along the bottom of the ocean, spearing fish, octopus, squid, and sea cucumbers while holding their breath for up to 5 minutes at a time. Meanwhile, the women gather sea urchins, sea cucumbers, and clams along the shore, and take a boat to a nearby market to sell them.

Children help their families fish, learning the skills as they grow. However, life at sea isn't all work, work, work. Bajau children have time to play, jumping from the walkways into the water and diving deep just for fun.

For Bajau people who live in houseboats, what often happens to them on land?

They get land sick.

How does fishing differ for Bajau men and women?

The men deep-sea dive for sea life and the women collect shellfish along the shore.

Write three sentences stating why you would or would not want to live like the Bajau people. Use key details from the text to support your answer.

Answers will vary.

BONUS: The gulls are scavengers by nature. When people moved into the birds' territory, birds adapted by learning to scavenge for discarded food scraps. Now they've moved inland to follow the new source of food.

page 30

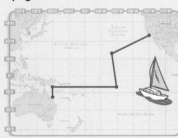

BONUS: forward a day

page 31

The writer Isak Dinesen once said, "The cure for anything is saltwater—sweat, tears, or the sea."

The captain pointed upward and said, "Red sky at night, sailors' delight; red sky at morning, sailors take warning."

I patted my brother on the back and said, "Well, there are plenty of other fish in the sea."

The shark poster said, "Reading is jawsome!"

The mermaid advised Marlin, "Just keep swimming!"

"How inappropriate to call this planet Earth," wrote Arthur C. Clarke, "when it is clearly Ocean."

Poet Anne Stevenson wrote, "The sea is as near as we come to another world."

"Remember," said the nature guide, "sand dollars are living creatures, not souvenirs."

Grandma always says, "Wait an hour after eating to go swimming."

page 32

inclined planes

levers

wedges

pulleys

screws

wheels and axles

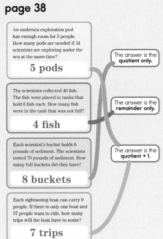

BONUS: a lever

pages 34–35

T	$33 \times 6 = 198$
H	$127 \times 2 = 254$
L	$2,345 \times 3 = 7,035$
I	$3,242 \times 3 = 9,726$
B	$60 \times 60 = 3,600$
C	$417 \times 4 = 1,668$
P	$651 \times 3 = 1,953$
G	$856 \times 5 = 4,280$
O	$76 \times 9 = 684$
S	$64 \times 5 = 320$
D	$2,316 \times 4 = 9,264$
W	$78 \times 2 = 156$
E	$78 \times 24 = 1,872$
U	$467 \times 4 = 1,868$
R	$170 \times 9 = 1,530$
F	$48 \times 53 = 2,544$
A	$19 \times 22 = 418$

Because he is claws-trophobic

page 36

Texas, Louisiana, Mississippi, Alabama, Florida

Utah, Colorado, Arizona, New Mexico

New Mexico, Oklahoma, Arkansas, Louisiana

Tennessee

Maine

page 37

page 38

An undersea exploration pod has enough room for 3 people. How many pods are needed if 14 scientists are exploring under the sea at the same time?

5 pods

The scientists collected 46 fish. The fish were placed in tanks that hold 6 fish each. How many fish were in the tank that was not full?

4 fish

Each scientist's bucket holds 8 pounds of sediment. The scientists tested 70 pounds of sediment. How many full buckets did they have?

8 buckets

Each sightseeing boat can carry 9 people. If there is only one boat and 57 people want to ride, how many trips will the boat have to make?

7 trips

The answer is the quotient only.

The answer is the remainder only.

The answer is the quotient + 1.

page 39

"I heard you have the freshest lobster on the wharf and the cheesiest grits around."

"We do have the freshest lobster, but we sold out of it."

"Then I'll have the catch of the day, a side of grits, and fried green tomatoes, because I'm very hungry."

"Would you like a bottle of water or root beer while you wait?"

"I'll take root beer, unless it has caffeine."

"It does not, so here you go. And here are your scuba gear and net."

"Scuba gear? Net? Although I love to scuba dive, I came here to eat, not swim."

"Well, our fisherman is out sick, so if you want the catch of the day, you have to catch it."

"Fine. I will catch the lobster. However, I only *eat* fresh seafood. I hope that I'm not expected to *cook* it, too."

BONUS: Answers will vary.

page 41

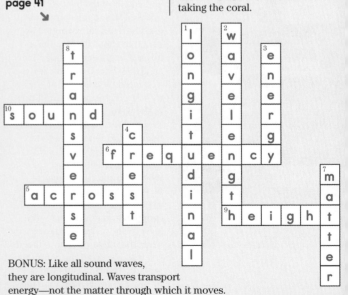

BONUS: Like all sound waves, they are longitudinal. Waves transport energy—not the matter through which it moves.

page 42

12	16		
19	28	15	101
159	143	214	112 r3

page 43

12 firefish

36 gobies

37 flounders

27 parrotfish

304 plankton

BONUS: 19 starfish

page 45

Shipwreck Park in Coral City has several broken slides. Who should fix them?

local government

Sharkansas's Waterway 62 has become crowded and needs more lanes. Who should rebuild the waterway?

state government

Planktown needs a new elementary school. Who should build it?

local government

It's time for mermaids to pay their income taxes. Who should collect the taxes?

federal government

The state of New Fishire is in debt and may raise the state sales tax. Who can authorize this?

state government

Mermaindy has declared war on the United States of Mermaids. Who will lead the military in this war?

federal government

BONUS: Answers will vary. Samples:

The state and local police could issue tickets to offenders.

The federal government could make it illegal to carry coral out of the country.

Any level of government could start an ad campaign discouraging people from taking the coral.

LEVEL 4A

page 49

amphibious
aquarium
telephone
thalassophobia
biology
photosynthesis
thermometer
ambience

page 50

BONUS: Answers will vary. Sample: So they could be reached by ships and trade.

page 51

The pacific ocean is the largest and the deepest of the five world oceans.

Cold Øcean water is more nutrient rich than warm ocean water, resulting in more sea life.

Storms off the coast of portugal can create massive waves, like the 100-foot one surfed by world record holder garrett mcnamara.

Penguins are often paired with polar bears in illustrations, but in fact, polar bears swim in the arctic ocean, and penguins in the antarctic ocean.

The phytoplankton and zooplankton in cold water make it look murky, whereas warm water is often Crystal clear.

The fastest fish in the ocean is the Sailfish, which has been clocked at 68 miles per hour.

Visit Vaadhoo Island, near india, and you may see the ocean glowing bright blue because of bioluminescent phytoplankton.

page 52

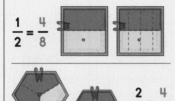

$$\frac{1}{2} = \frac{4}{8}$$

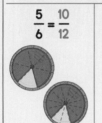

$$\frac{2}{3} = \frac{4}{6}$$

$$\frac{5}{6} = \frac{10}{12}$$

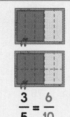

$$\frac{3}{5} = \frac{6}{10}$$

page 53

$$\frac{1}{3} = \frac{2}{6} = \frac{4}{12}$$

$$\frac{1}{4} = \frac{2}{8} = \frac{3}{12}$$

$$\frac{1}{2} = \frac{2}{4} = \frac{3}{6} = \frac{4}{8} = \frac{5}{10} = \frac{6}{12}$$

BONUS: $\frac{2}{10}$

page 55

lakeside
sloop's
choppy
fjord
paddled
estuary
yacht
shaggy
glided

page 56

LEVEL 4B

page 58

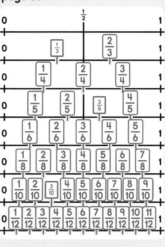

page 59

$\frac{5}{8}$, because it is greater than $\frac{1}{2}$, and $\frac{4}{12}$ is less than $\frac{1}{2}$ on the number line.

page 60

Answers will vary.

 CO_2
↓
phytoplankton
↓
zooplankton
↓
larger animal, such as a shrimp
↓
larger animal, such as a tuna
↓
animals at the top of the food chain, such as sharks

page 61

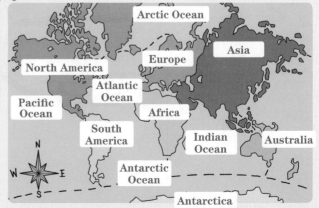

pages 62–63

Answers will vary. Samples:

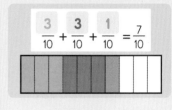
$$\frac{3}{10} + \frac{3}{10} + \frac{1}{10} = \frac{7}{10}$$

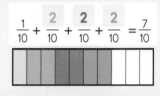
$$\frac{1}{10} + \frac{2}{10} + \frac{2}{10} + \frac{2}{10} = \frac{7}{10}$$

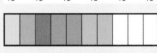
$$\frac{1}{10} + \frac{1}{10} + \frac{1}{10} + \frac{2}{10} + \frac{2}{10} = \frac{7}{10}$$

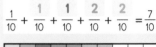

Answers will vary. Samples:

$$\frac{7}{8} = \frac{2}{8} + \frac{2}{8} + \frac{3}{8}$$

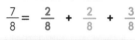

$$\frac{7}{8} = \frac{4}{8} + \frac{2}{8} + \frac{1}{8}$$

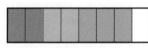

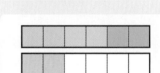

$$\frac{8}{6} = \frac{2}{6} + \frac{2}{6} + \frac{2}{6} + \frac{2}{6}$$

BONUS: Answers will vary.

page 64

Cleaning out the garage seemed as daunting as counting the grains of sand on the beach. **S**

Everyone knew David was bullying Chris, but when it came to being suspended, David was as slippery as an eel. **S**

In the lemonade-stand business, Ceresa was a real shark. **M**

By the end of lessons, Luke could swim like a fish. **S**

Sea lions are the dogs of the sea. **M**

Cora's dream of a beach vacation was like a mermaid: lovely but not real. **S**

After placing second in her surfing competition, Wendy cried an ocean of tears. **M**

Answers will vary.

page 66

$\frac{5}{3} = \frac{3}{3} + \frac{2}{3} = 1 + \frac{2}{3} = 1\frac{2}{3}$

$\frac{7}{4} = \frac{4}{4} + \frac{3}{4} = 1 + \frac{3}{4} = 1\frac{3}{4}$

$\frac{11}{5} = \frac{5}{5} + \frac{5}{5} + \frac{1}{5} = 2 + \frac{1}{5} = 2\frac{1}{5}$

$\frac{10}{3} = \frac{3}{3} + \frac{3}{3} + \frac{3}{3} + \frac{1}{3} = 3 + \frac{1}{3} = 3\frac{1}{3}$

$\frac{20}{8} = \frac{8}{8} + \frac{8}{8} + \frac{4}{8} = 2 + \frac{4}{8} = 2\frac{4}{8}$

$1\frac{1}{4} = \frac{4}{4} + \frac{1}{4} = \frac{5}{4}$

$2\frac{3}{10} = \frac{10}{10} + \frac{10}{10} + \frac{3}{10} = \frac{23}{10}$

$1\frac{7}{12} = \frac{12}{12} + \frac{7}{12} = \frac{19}{12}$

$3\frac{5}{8} = \frac{8}{8} + \frac{8}{8} + \frac{8}{8} + \frac{5}{8} = \frac{29}{8}$

$2\frac{3}{4} = \frac{4}{4} + \frac{4}{4} + \frac{3}{4} = \frac{11}{4}$

LEVEL 5A

page 68

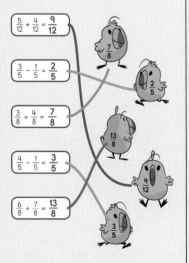

$\frac{5}{12} + \frac{4}{12} = \frac{9}{12}$

$\frac{3}{5} - \frac{1}{5} = \frac{2}{5}$

$\frac{3}{8} + \frac{4}{8} = \frac{7}{8}$

$\frac{4}{5} - \frac{1}{5} = \frac{3}{5}$

$\frac{6}{8} + \frac{7}{8} = \frac{13}{8}$

page 69

Yes

during a waning gibbous moon

swollen on one side

The sun lights the moon on the side that we cannot see.

page 70

Minnesota

the Gulf of Mexico

the Arkansas River

Tennessee or Mississippi

Minnesota, Wisconsin, Iowa, Illinois, Missouri, Kentucky, Arkansas, Tennessee, Mississippi, and Louisiana

page 71

Answers will vary.

ice that extends on land for at least 20,000 square miles (50,000 square kilometers) **ice sheet**	a layer of soil beneath the surface that remains frozen **permafrost**
a river of ice that is slowly moving under its own weight **glacier**	ice that has broken off from a glacier and is floating in the water **iceberg**

page 72

$2\frac{1}{4} + 1\frac{3}{4} = \frac{9}{4} + \frac{7}{4} = \frac{16}{4} = $ **4**

$3\frac{1}{3} + 1\frac{2}{3} = \frac{10}{3} + \frac{5}{3} = \frac{15}{3} = $ **5**

$4\frac{2}{5} - \frac{4}{5} = \frac{22}{5} - \frac{4}{5} = \frac{18}{5} = $ **$3\frac{3}{5}$**

$1\frac{4}{10} + 1\frac{9}{10} = \frac{14}{10} + \frac{19}{10} = \frac{33}{10} = $ **$3\frac{3}{10}$**

$3\frac{2}{6} - 1\frac{5}{6} = \frac{20}{6} - \frac{11}{6} = \frac{9}{6} = $ **$1\frac{3}{6}$**

$\frac{4}{8}$ meters

page 73

$3\frac{1}{2} + 2\frac{1}{2} = $ **6**

$2\frac{2}{3} + 2\frac{2}{3} = $ **$5\frac{1}{3}$**

$3\frac{2}{6} - 2\frac{3}{6} = $ **$\frac{5}{6}$**

$4\frac{2}{5} - 1\frac{4}{5} = $ **$2\frac{3}{5}$**

$2\frac{3}{12} - 1\frac{8}{12} = $ **$\frac{7}{12}$**

$1\frac{6}{8} + 2\frac{7}{8} = $ **$4\frac{5}{8}$**

You sail with a friend for $2\frac{1}{4}$ hours. Then you swim for $\frac{2}{4}$ hour. How much time in all did you spend swimming and sailing? **$3\frac{2}{4}$ hours**

page 74

earthquake
new mountain

earthquake
volcano

earthquake
volcano

earthquake

page 75

T
F
T
T
F

BONUS: The land had been underwater at one time.

pages 76–77

$3 \times \frac{1}{2} = \frac{3}{2}$ or $1\frac{1}{2}$

$7 \times \frac{1}{3} = \frac{7}{3}$ or $2\frac{1}{3}$

$4 \times \frac{5}{6} = \frac{20}{6}$ or $3\frac{2}{6}$

$6 \times \frac{2}{3} = \frac{12}{3}$ or 4

$7 \times \frac{3}{8} = \frac{21}{8}$ or $2\frac{5}{8}$

$5 \times \frac{3}{10} = \frac{15}{10}$ or $1\frac{5}{10}$

$10 \times \frac{2}{4} = \frac{20}{4}$ or 5

$3 \times \frac{7}{12} = \frac{21}{12}$ or $1\frac{9}{12}$

$13 \times \frac{7}{8} = \frac{91}{8}$ or $11\frac{3}{8}$

$\frac{28}{3}$ or $9\frac{1}{3}$ cups

$\frac{9}{4}$ or $2\frac{1}{4}$ buckets

page 78

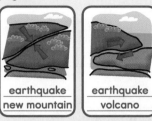

He (the King of Great Britain) has refused his assent to laws, the most wholesome and necessary for the public good. — The King won't allow necessary laws to be passed in the colonies.

He has kept among us, in times of peace, Standing Armies without the Consent of our legislatures. — Colonists are being punished for alleged crimes without ever being given a jury trial.

For Quartering large bodies of armed troops among us. — The King has sent his army to patrol the colonies, against their will, though it is not wartime.

For protecting them (soldiers), by a mock Trial, from punishment for any Murders which they should commit on the Inhabitants of these States. — The King allows his troops to live in the homes of colonists without their permission.

For depriving us in many cases, of the benefits of Trial by Jury. — When soldiers are accused of murdering colonists, they are put on trial, but it is only for show; the soldiers are always declared innocent.

BONUS: Answers will vary. Sample: The king won't let the colonies trade goods with other nations.

page 79

Dear Ms. Shelly Delray:
Please consider me for the open position at Shelly's Snack Shack. I have good people skills, and I love talking to people. I **also** love to cook and have experience making sandwiches and snacks. **Although** I have never worked at a snack bar, I baby-sat all last summer and made breakfast and lunch for the kids every day. I did this in a very hectic environment. **For example/ For instance**, I once had to make five peanut butter sandwiches while breaking up a fight between twin toddlers. **In other words**, I am well prepared for even the busiest of days at Shelly's Snack Shack. I can start May 25.

Thank you,
Matthew Craig

page 80

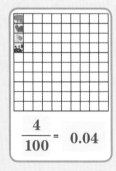

$\frac{75}{100} = 0.75$

$\frac{4}{100} = 0.04$

$\frac{29}{100} = 0.29$ $\frac{46}{100} = 0.46$ $\frac{87}{100} = 0.87$

$\frac{3}{100} = 0.03$ $\frac{30}{100} = 0.3$ $\frac{98}{100} = 0.98$

$0.02 = \frac{2}{100}$ $0.45 = \frac{45}{100}$ $0.6 = \frac{60}{100}$ or $\frac{6}{10}$

LEVEL 5B

page 84

Will a peeled orange or unpeeled orange float?

The peeled orange will float, and the unpeeled orange will not.

I placed an unpeeled orange in a bowl of water and a peeled orange in a bowl of water. Both oranges were the same size, and both bowls had the same amount of water.

The peeled orange sank, and the unpeeled orange floated.

No, the hypothesis was not correct.

BONUS: Answers will vary. Sample: Jellyfish thrive in warmer water.

page 90

The skua seabird flies menacingly <u>over the penguins</u>.
The penguins dive <u>under the iceberg</u>.
The iceberg floats <u>alongside our ship</u>.
The ship sails <u>beside a family of whales</u>.
<u>During high tide</u>, a whale becomes stranded <u>on the beach</u>.
We work <u>through the night</u> to save the whale.
<u>As night turns into day</u>, we launch the creature <u>into the bay</u>.
<u>Beyond the bay</u>, the whale's pod waits for it.
Answers will vary.

page 91

Last summer, my mom rented a beach house for the whole summer. I was so excited! But when we <u>get</u> there, it <u>is</u> an abandoned shack. The windows were broken, the weeds were overgrown, and sand was everywhere.

My mom called the owner to complain, but no one answered. She asked a neighbor if there was another number where we could reach him. The neighbor <u>says</u> the owner <u>has</u> been dead for five years. Then how was my mom able to talk to him in the first place? Gulp!

Since we couldn't figure out how to get our money back, we <u>decide</u> to clean the house and fix the windows. It took all week! While my mom and I were cleaning the yard, a girl my age rode her bike past us. I waved hello, but she didn't wave back.

"Who are you waving to?" my mom <u>asks</u>.

"That girl riding her bike in the street," I <u>say</u>.

"Abi," my mom said. "There is no girl in the street."

A chill went down my back. What was going on here? And <u>do</u> I have the courage to find out?

got
was
said
had
decided
asked
said
did

page 92

Amendment VI
Amendment I
Amendment IV

page 93

90°
70°
20°
40°

BONUS: Answers will vary. Sample: The mouth opening looks larger than the top fish on this page that is 90°, so the puffer fish's smile is greater than 90°.

LEVEL 6A

page 96

obtuse   right

acute

obtuse

acute

right

page 97

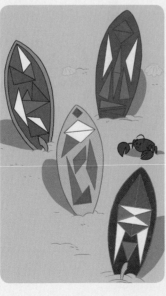

page 99

~~The Industrial Revolution led to a new way of life for everyone.~~ <u>In preindustrial America, small farms provided a living for many families. During the Industrial Revolution, farming practices and machines became more efficient, leading to greater food production.</u> More abundant food led to better health, which in turn lowered the death rate and raised the birth rate.

~~Meanwhile, with the invention of water-powered machines, large factories replaced the small shops in which workers once built products from start to finish.~~ The factories provided jobs to the nation's growing population. (Unfortunately, the workers endured long hours for low pay under dangerous conditions.)

(Moreover, as towns and cities grew up around the factories, overcrowding became an issue and diseases became rampant.) Anxious to stop the suffering, doctors researched the causes of the diseases, and learned that many spread through dirty water. Armed with this knowledge, cities created sanitary sewage systems. (Other changes in living conditions were slower to come about, and sickness was still a problem.) However, the improved technology of the Industrial Revolution had set in motion advances that would lead to better health care and a higher quality of life in the industrial world. (Unfortunately, it also introduced a new public health concern: the air pollution caused by burning fossil fuels, such as coal, oil, and natural gas, to produce electricity and power factories.)

page 100

page 101

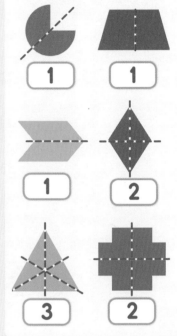

1   1

1   2

3   2

page 103

	Cactus	Evergreen
Narrow, adapted leaves result in reduced water loss.	✓	✓
Adapted leaves have features that repel animals.	✓	✓
Leaves are shed each fall.		
Photosynthesis occurs in the stem rather than in the leaves.	✓	
A waxy coating on the plant prevents water loss.	✓	✓
The plant has a cone shape.		✓
The stem stores water.	✓	
Flowers attract animals for pollination.	✓	
Pollination occurs through wind only.		✓

page 104

$3 + 7 - 5 = 5$
$5 \times 2 + 7 = 17$
$5 \times (2 + 7) = 45$
$(4 + 6) \times 2 = 20$
$25 \div 5 + 6 = 11$
$20 \div (10 - 5) = 4$
$20 - 12 \div 2 = 14$
$3 \times 6 + 4 \times 2 = 26$
$10 \times 6 - 50 = 10$

page 105

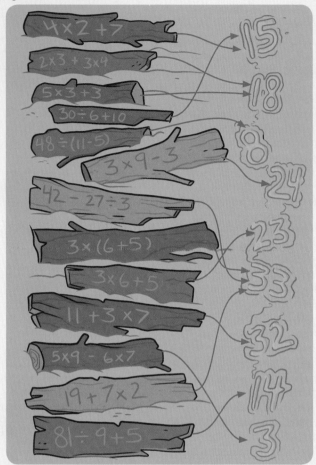

page 106

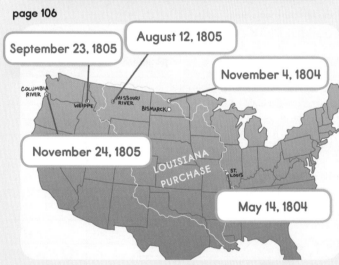

September 23, 1805

August 12, 1805

November 4, 1804

November 24, 1805

May 14, 1804

COLUMBIA RIVER
WEIPPE
MISSOURI RIVER
BISMARCK
LOUISIANA PURCHASE
ST. LOUIS

page 108

Seven tenths 0.7

Seven hundredths 0.07

Seven thousandths 0.007

Thirteen hundredths 0.13

Three hundred twelve thousandths 0.312

Seven and twelve hundredths 7.12

Two and one hundred nine thousandths 2.109

$\frac{3}{10} + \frac{9}{100}$ 0.39

$\frac{1}{10} + \frac{4}{100}$ 0.14

$\frac{3}{10} + \frac{9}{100} + \frac{7}{1000}$ 0.397

$2 + \frac{6}{10} + \frac{2}{100} + \frac{1}{1000}$ 2.621

page 109

1.486 > 1.386

0.40 = 0.400

5.612 > 5.016

0.529 < 0.922

0.427 > 0.421

5.05 < 5.052

0.880 > 0.808

7.545 > 7.445

0.489 < 0.582

10.02 = 10.020

0.045 < 0.054

0.599 < 0.6

Answers will vary. Samples:
0.999, 0.978, 0.989

Answers will vary. Samples:
0.888, 0.800, 0.799

0.219, 0.220, 0.221

BONUS: 1.025 < 1.205 and
1.205 > 1.025

page 110

5 × 10 = 50

6 × 100 = 600

7 × 1,000 = 7,000

3 × 40 = 120

4 × 600 = 2,400

5 × 5,000 = 25,000

20 × 60 = 1,200

LEVEL 6B

page 114

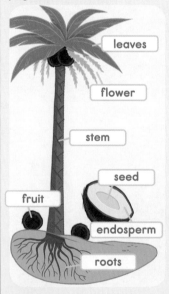

leaves

flower

stem

seed

fruit

endosperm

roots

BONUS: They floated across the ocean.

page 115

84,637 rounded to the nearest thousand is 85,000.

The largest number is 144 centimeters, and the smallest number is 135 centimeters.

Answers will vary but may include:

2,200: I rounded 97 to 100 and multiplied by 22.

1,940 shells: I rounded 22 to 20 and multiplied by 97.

2,000 shells: I rounded 22 to 20 and 97 to 100, and multiplied 20 × 100.

215,754 rounded to the nearest ten thousand is 220,000.

Answers will vary. Samples:

First way, Round 12 to 10 and multiply 10 × 15, which equals 150.

Second way: Round 15 to 20 and multiply 12 × 20, which equals 240.

The first way is more accurate because 12 is closer to 10 than 15 is to 20.

page 116

Answers will vary but may include:
seasickness
sand in coffee
salt in tea
fishy taste in eggs
no plants
wet feet

. . . If you like your coffee
    with sand for dregs,
A decided hint of salt in
    your tea,
And a fishy taste in the
    very eggs—
By all means choose the Sea.

Lines 1 and 3 rhyme, and lines 2 and 4 rhyme

page 119

The explorers saw several arctic foxes.

The number of hours the ship had sailed from Brattahlid to the Western Settlement and then to Bear Island; or the geography of the islands described.

Answers will vary. Samples: seeds, livestock, fishing nets, axes, knives, barrels of water, prepared foods, blankets, cloth, paper, pens, medicine, gifts for natives of the land

Answers will vary.

page 120

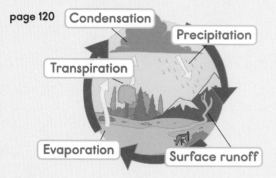

Condensation

Precipitation

Transpiration

Evaporation

Surface runoff

page 121

Body of Water	Percentage of the World's Water
Ocean	**97%**
Glacier	**2%**
Groundwater, freshwater lakes, saltwater lakes, inland seas, the atmosphere, and rivers	**less than 1%**

page 123

Answers will vary. Sample: The Little Mermaid is the most beautiful of all her sisters, and she is quiet and thoughtful.

Answers will vary. Sample: It is a beautiful place deep underwater, built with coral and shells.

The flowers are fragrant, the trees are green, the "fishes" or birds sing.

The Little Mermaid falls in love with a statue of a boy.

Sometimes in yearning for what we don't have, we take for granted the things that we do have.

Answers will vary.

page 124

$\frac{4}{6}$ fathoms

$1\frac{1}{6}$ fathoms

$\frac{4}{6} - \frac{2}{6} = \frac{2}{6}$ fathoms difference

$1\frac{1}{6} - \frac{2}{6} = \frac{7}{6} - \frac{2}{6} = \frac{5}{6}$ fathoms difference

$2 \times 1\frac{1}{6} = 2 \times \frac{7}{6} = \frac{14}{6} = 2\frac{2}{6}$ fathoms

Summer Brain Quest Extras

Stay smart all summer long with these Summer Brain Quest Extras! In this section you'll find:

Summer Brain Quest Reading List

A book can take you anywhere—and summer is a great time to go on a reading adventure! Use the Summer Brain Quest Reading List to help you start the next chapter of your quest!

Summer Brain Quest Mini Deck

Cut out the cards and make your own Summer Brain Quest Mini Deck. Play by yourself or with a friend, or stump a parent or family member!

Summer Brain Quest Reading List

We recommend reading at least 15 to 30 minutes each day. Read to yourself or aloud. You can also read aloud with a friend or family member and discuss the book. Here are some questions to get you started:

- Was the book a nonfiction (informational) or fiction (story/narrative) text?
- Who or what was the book about?
- What was the setting of the story (where did it take place)?
- Was there a main character? Who was it? Describe the character.
- Was there a problem in the story? What was it? How was it solved?
- Were there any themes in the story? What were they? How do you know?
- Were there any lessons in the story? What were they? How do you know?
- Why do you think the author wrote the book?

Jump-start your reading adventure by visiting your local library or bookstore and checking out the following books. Track which ones you've read, and write your own review! Would you recommend this book to a friend? If so, which friend would you recommend this book to, and why?

Fiction

Black Ships Before Troy: The Story of The Iliad, by Rosemary Sutcliff

This retelling of the epic poem *The Iliad* has an adventure story for everyone, from abductions to combat and from indescribable beauty to godly meddling.

DATE STARTED: _____ DATE FINISHED: _____

MY REVIEW: _____

_____

Blubber, by Judy Blume

It all starts when Linda gives an oral report on a whale. Jill and Wendy won't stop teasing her, and it doesn't take long for the rest of the class to join in. Until the tables turn and Jill finds herself on the receiving end of the bullying instead . . .

DATE STARTED: _____ DATE FINISHED: _____

MY REVIEW: _____

_____

Bluffton: My Summers with Buster Keaton, written and illustrated by Matt Phelan

It's the year 1908, and a troupe of vaudeville performers has taken the sleepy town of Muskegon, Michigan, by storm.

DATE STARTED: _____ DATE FINISHED: _____

MY REVIEW: _____

_____

How Tia Lola Saved the Summer, by Julia Alvarez

Miguel Guzman isn't looking forward to summer. Between his annoying family friends crashing in the living room and a baseball injury, it's lucky that Tia Lola is here to save the day with a magical summer camp!

DATE STARTED: _____ DATE FINISHED: _____

MY REVIEW: _____

_____

Island of the Blue Dolphins, by Scott O'Dell

When Karana's Native American tribe is forced to leave their island by Russian fur hunters, she and her brother miss the ship and get left behind. How will they survive alone on the island?

DATE STARTED: _____ DATE FINISHED: _____

MY REVIEW: _____

_____

The Liberation of Gabriel King, by K. L. Going

Gabriel King is scared of a lot of things—spiders, killer robots, and loose cows, for starters. His best friend Frita, as the only black kid in a town with an active Ku Klux Klan, knows more than a thing or two about being scared. This summer, they both face their fears.

DATE STARTED: _____ DATE FINISHED: _____

MY REVIEW: _____

_____

The Miraculous Journey of Edward Tulane, written by Kate DiCamillo, illustrated by Bagram Ibatoulline

One minute, Edward Tulane is a china rabbit adored by his mistress Abilene in their beautiful house on Egypt Street. The next, he's lost, launched into a journey across the globe to find his way home.

DATE STARTED: _____ DATE FINISHED: _____

MY REVIEW: _____

_____

The Book of Storms, by Ruth Hatfield

After a major thunderstorm, eleven-year-old Danny wakes up to an empty house. His storm-chasing parents are gone, and the giant sycamore in his backyard has been destroyed. When he picks up a piece of the shattered tree, he discovers he can communicate with the natural world!

DATE STARTED: _____ DATE FINISHED: _____

MY REVIEW: _____

_____

Serafina's Promise, by Ann E. Burg

Serafina lives in Port-au-Prince, Haiti. Though she dreams of going to school and becoming a doctor, she has more urgent family responsibilities. It's hard to imagine a world beyond the poverty she lives in, and then, the 2010 earthquake strikes. . . .

DATE STARTED: _____ DATE FINISHED: _____

MY REVIEW: _____

_____

The Crossover, by Kwame Alexander

Twin brothers Josh and Jordan Bell are middle-school basketball stars. They used to be close, but now that Jordan is dating the new girl, they don't spend as much time together. Josh relays his family's story on and off the court in beats: "Stop all that quivering. Cuz tonight I'm delivering."

DATE STARTED: _____ DATE FINISHED: _____

MY REVIEW: _____

_____

Nonfiction

Almost Astronauts: 13 Women Who Dared to Dream,
by Tanya Lee Stone

Even though this group of women passed every test required to become astronauts, NASA refused them the opportunity because of their gender. Read about their inspiring courage and determination.

DATE STARTED: _____   DATE FINISHED: _____

MY REVIEW: _____

_____

World Without Fish, written by Mark Kurlansky, illustrated by Frank Stockton

The fish we most commonly eat, like tuna and salmon, are disappearing so quickly that they could go extinct within fifty years. Learn about what's happening to the world's oceans and what you can do about it.

DATE STARTED: _____   DATE FINISHED: _____

MY REVIEW: _____

_____

The Fairy Ring: Or Elsie and Frances Fool the World, by Mary Losure

In the early 1900s, cousins Elsie and Frances took pictures of painted paper fairies. The photos, meant to be lighthearted fun, ended up tricking a world of accomplished adults into believing the creatures were real!

DATE STARTED: _____ DATE FINISHED: _____

MY REVIEW: _____

_____

A Girl Called Vincent: The Life of Poet Edna St. Vincent Millay, by Krystyna Poray Goddu

Follow Edna St. Vincent Millay, one of the most important American poets of the Jazz Age, from a little cabin in rural Maine to her acceptance of the Pulitzer Prize.

DATE STARTED: _____ DATE FINISHED: _____

MY REVIEW: _____

_____

GO: A Kidd's Guide to Graphic Design, written by Chip Kidd, photographed by Geoff Spear

When designers communicate their ideas to the world, they pull out all the stops—form, line, color, scale. Delve into a designer's imagination and see the world in a whole new way.

DATE STARTED: _____ DATE FINISHED: _____

MY REVIEW: _____

_____

How to Turn $100 into $1,000,000: Earn! Invest! Save!, by James McKenna and Jeannine Glista, with Matt Fontaine

From investing in stocks to inventing antigravity popcorn, learn how to be money-smart with this easy-to-follow book.

DATE STARTED: _____   DATE FINISHED: _____

MY REVIEW: _____

_____

Neighborhood Sharks: Hunting with the Great Whites of California's Farallon Islands, written and illustrated by Katherine Roy

Follow the great white sharks in their migration to find seal meals.

DATE STARTED: _____   DATE FINISHED: _____

MY REVIEW: _____

_____

The Port Chicago 50: Disaster, Mutiny, and the Fight for Civil Rights, by Steve Sheinkin

When an explosion killed more than 300 men at a naval base, a protest of its dangerous racial segregation was ignited.

DATE STARTED: _____   DATE FINISHED: _____

MY REVIEW: _____

_____

Secrets of a Civil War Submarine: Solving the Mysteries of the **H. L. Hunley**, by Sally M. Walker

After making history as the first submarine to sink a ship in battle, the *H. L. Hunley* disappeared. Over 130 years later, it was discovered buried off the coast of South Carolina. Uncover its secrets!

DATE STARTED: _____   DATE FINISHED: _____

MY REVIEW: _____

_____

Tracking Trash: Flotsam, Jetsam, and the Science of Ocean Motion, by Loree Griffin Burns

Learn about the ocean's currents by tracking trash, from sneakers to bath toys, across the Pacific Ocean.

DATE STARTED: _____   DATE FINISHED: _____

MY REVIEW: _____

_____

And don't stop here! There's a whole world to discover. All you need is a book!

Summer Brain Quest Mini Deck

QUESTIONS

 Find the relative adverb in this sentence: "That's the reason why I'm afraid of birds."

 What is the mixture of mud and straw that is used to build homes and buildings called?

 What percentage of Earth's water is salt water: 14 percent, 53 percent, or 97 percent?

 You find 5,000 pieces of silver in a treasure chest and divide them into 50 equal bags. How many coins will be in each bag?

QUESTIONS

 Is "roared like a lion" a simile or metaphor?

 What was the first U.S. state?

 A drumstick (musical instrument) is an example of what simple machine?

 There were 2,177 fish in a school of fish and 2,700 fish in another school of fish. Which school had more fish?

QUESTIONS

 Find the progressive verb in this sentence: "I was building a sandcastle."

 Which state abbreviation contains an x?

 Which of these is a mineral? gold, lava, granite

 Sofia collected a number of seashells that can be expressed as 6,000 + 700 + 7. How many seashells is that?

QUESTIONS

 Does "overcast" mean cloudy or thrown too far?

 What state features the southernmost point in the United States?

 What causes summer in the Northern or Southern Hemisphere?

 Tom caught a bluefish that was 21 inches long. That is 3 times as long as the fish his brother caught. How long was Tom's brother's fish?

ANSWERS

 a simile

 Delaware

 a lever

 the school with 2,700 fish

ANSWERS

 why

 adobe

 97 percent

 100

ANSWERS

 cloudy

 Hawaii

 The earth's tilt. It's summer in the hemisphere tilted toward the sun at that time of year.

 7 inches

ANSWERS

 was building

 Texas—TX

 gold

 6,707

QUESTIONS

 In Greek mythology, who is the goddess of wisdom and war?

 Which river is on the border of Texas and Mexico?

 What is the boiling point of water in degrees Fahrenheit and Celsius?

 If someone enjoyed a lobster dinner 52 times a year, how many would he enjoy it in 7 years?

QUESTIONS

 "But," "or," and "because" are what parts of speech?

 In what year was the Declaration of Independence written?

 What force causes objects to fall toward the earth?

 There are 35 people going on a trip. If each van holds 8 passengers, how many vans are needed so everyone can go?

QUESTIONS

 Where is a comma needed in this sentence? "I'm freezing cold and soaking wet and I'm going home."

 What ocean is the farthest north on the globe?

 How many days does it take for the moon to cycle around the earth?

 Ellie saw 13 starfish. How many factors does the number 13 have?

QUESTIONS

 Does "hoity-toity" mean snobbish or upside down?

 What are the first 10 amendments of the Constitution known as?

 In which phase is more of the moon visible: waning gibbous or waxing crescent?

 What is the quotient if 117 seagulls are divided into 3 equal groups?

ANSWERS

 conjunctions

 1776

 gravity

 5 vans

ANSWERS

 Athena

 The Rio Grande

 212 degrees F, 100 degree C

 364

ANSWERS

 snobbish

 The Bill of Rights

 waning gibbous

 39

ANSWERS

 Between "wet" and "and"

 The Arctic Ocean

 29.5 days

 2 factors: 1 and 13

QUESTIONS

 Is the following sentence written in the first or third person? "Aiesha rowed as if her life depended on it."

 In what year was the Louisiana Purchase made? 1703, 1803, 1903

 When an organism such as a firefly lights up, what is it called?

 One-fourth of beach-goers are good swimmers. What is an equivalent fraction with 8 in the denominator?

QUESTIONS

 Is "mispelled" spelled correctly here?

 The Oregon Trail ended in Oregon and began in which state?

 What are the toothlike scales on sharks called?

 What equation shows how you can divide up 1 batch of tuna salad using unit fractions with 3 in the denominator?

QUESTIONS

 Which of the following is not a preposition? in, alongside, under, they

 What line running through North and South America separates rivers flowing into the Pacific Ocean from those flowing into the Atlantic Ocean?

 Instead of flowers, what do conifer trees have that allow them to reproduce?

 Which statement is correct:

$\frac{3}{8} < \frac{1}{2}$, $\frac{3}{8} = \frac{1}{2}$, $\frac{3}{8} > \frac{1}{2}$

QUESTIONS

 What part of speech is "Uh-oh!"?

 The Santa Fe Trail is named for its final destination, a city in which state?

 Herpetology is the study of what?

 Diana's little sister watched a mermaid cartoon $2\frac{1}{5}$ times before she fell asleep. What is $2\frac{1}{5}$ as an equivalent fraction?

160

ANSWERS

 No, it should be "misspelled."

 Missouri

 denticles

 $\frac{1}{3} + \frac{1}{3} + \frac{1}{3}$

ANSWERS

 third person

 1803

 bioluminescence

 $\frac{2}{8}$

ANSWERS

 an interjection

 New Mexico

 reptiles and amphibians

 $\frac{11}{5}$

ANSWERS

 they

 The Continental Divide or Great Divide

 pinecones

 $\frac{3}{8} < \frac{1}{2}$

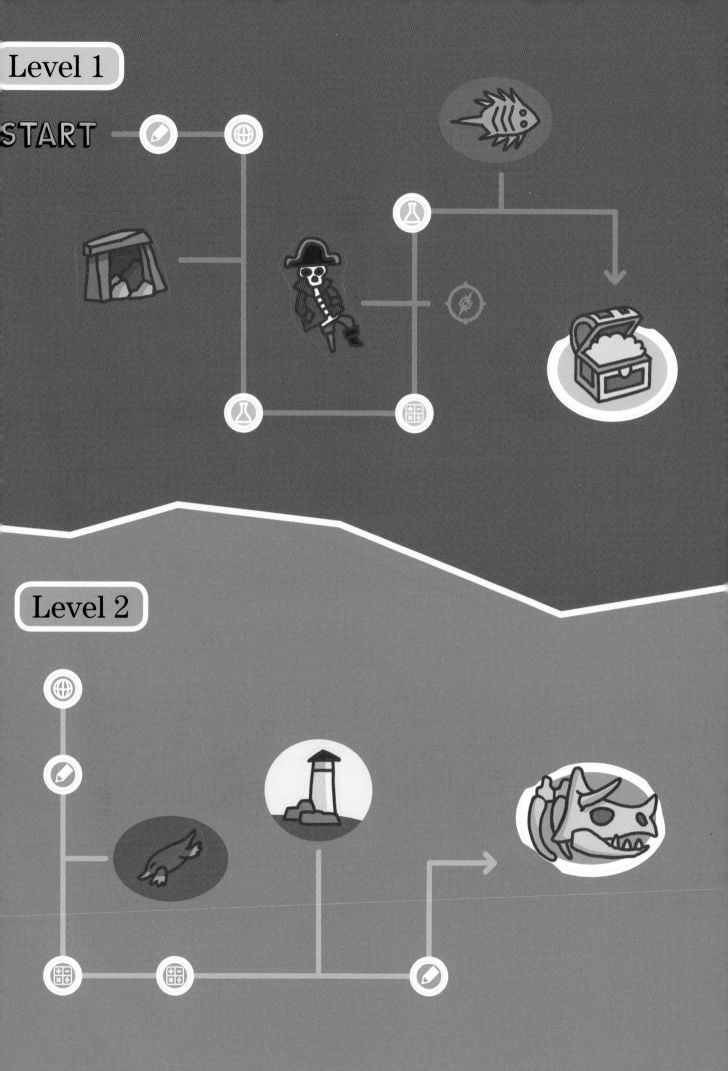

Level 1

START

Level 2

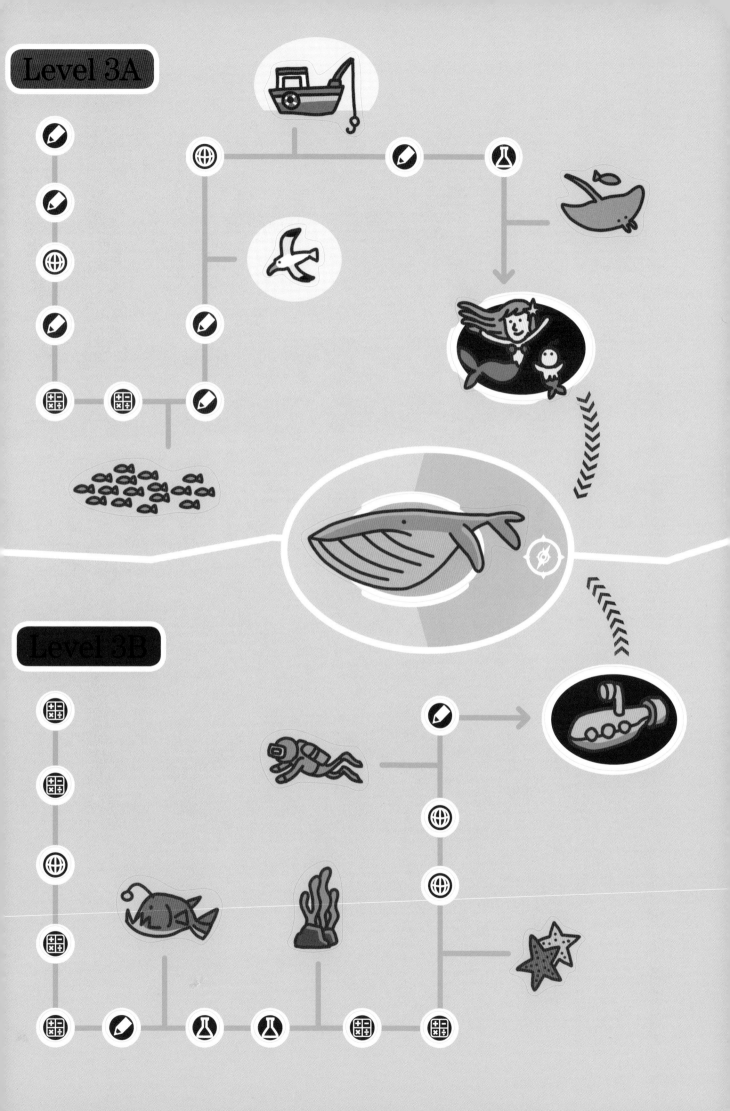

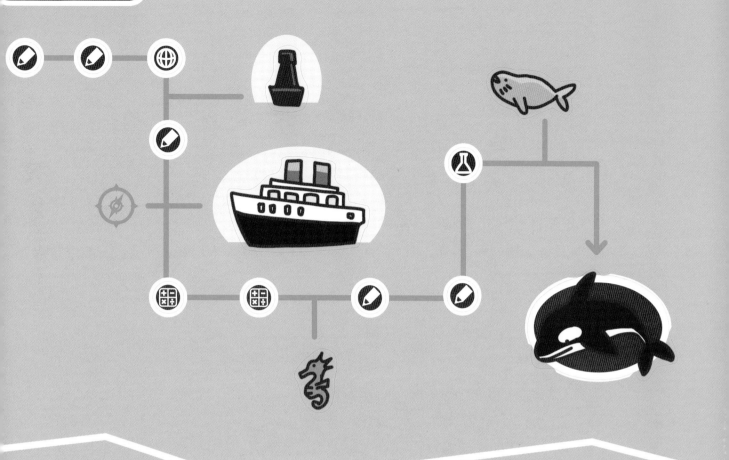

Level 4A

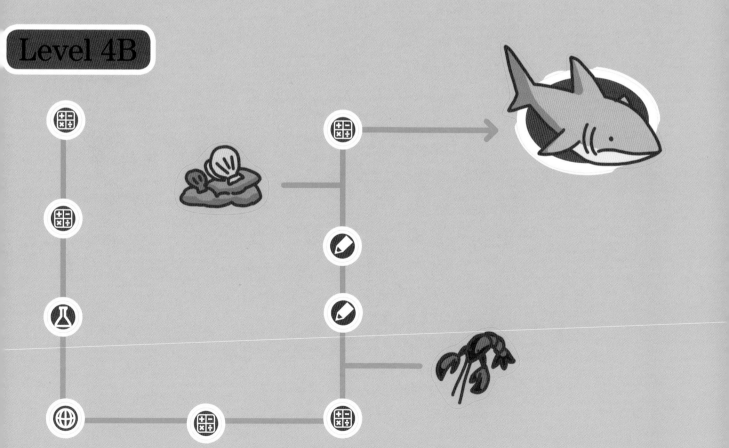

Level 4B

Level 5A

Level 5B

Level 6A

QUEST complete!
Welcome to
5th grade!

Turn the page to
get your QUEST
COMPLETE
sticker!

Level 6B

QUEST complete!
Welcome to 5th grade!

Did you sticker **every** route possible and finish **all** the Outside Quests? What an achievement!

You've earned the 100% STICKER!

SUMMER BRAIN QUEST®

Between Grades 4 & 5 Map Legend

- ⊞ Math page
- ⚗ Science page
- 🌐 Social studies page
- ✏ English language arts page
- ◈ Outside Quest

FINISH!

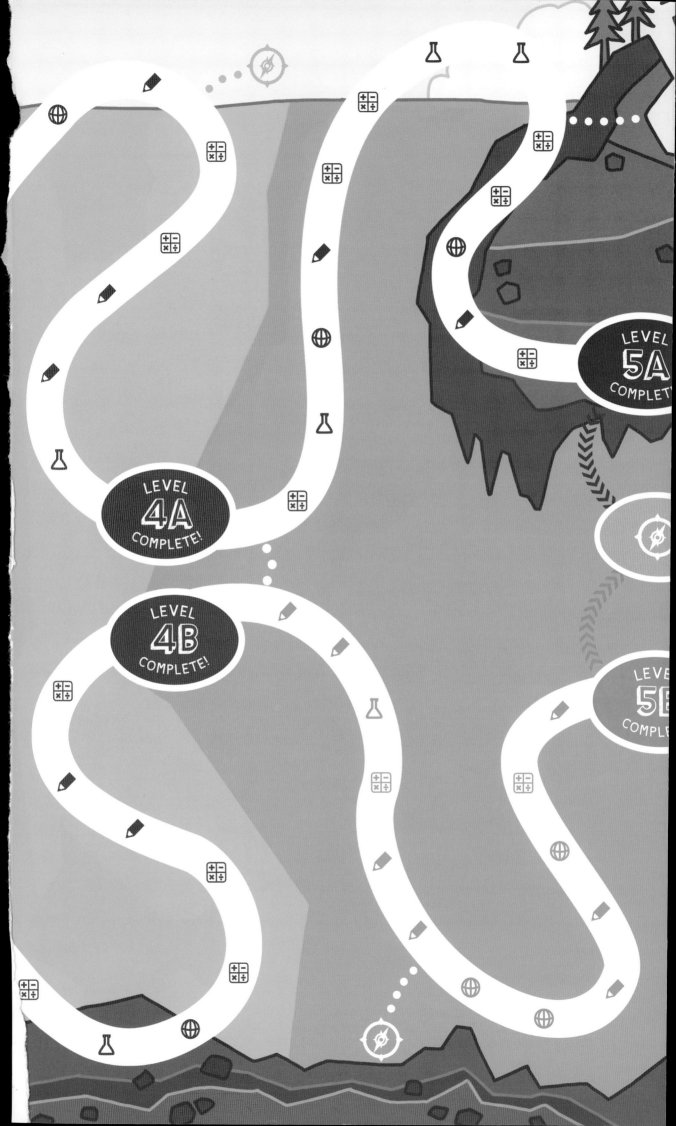

LEVEL
5A
COMPLET

LEVEL
4A
COMPLETE!

LEVEL
4B
COMPLETE!

LEVEL
5
COMPL

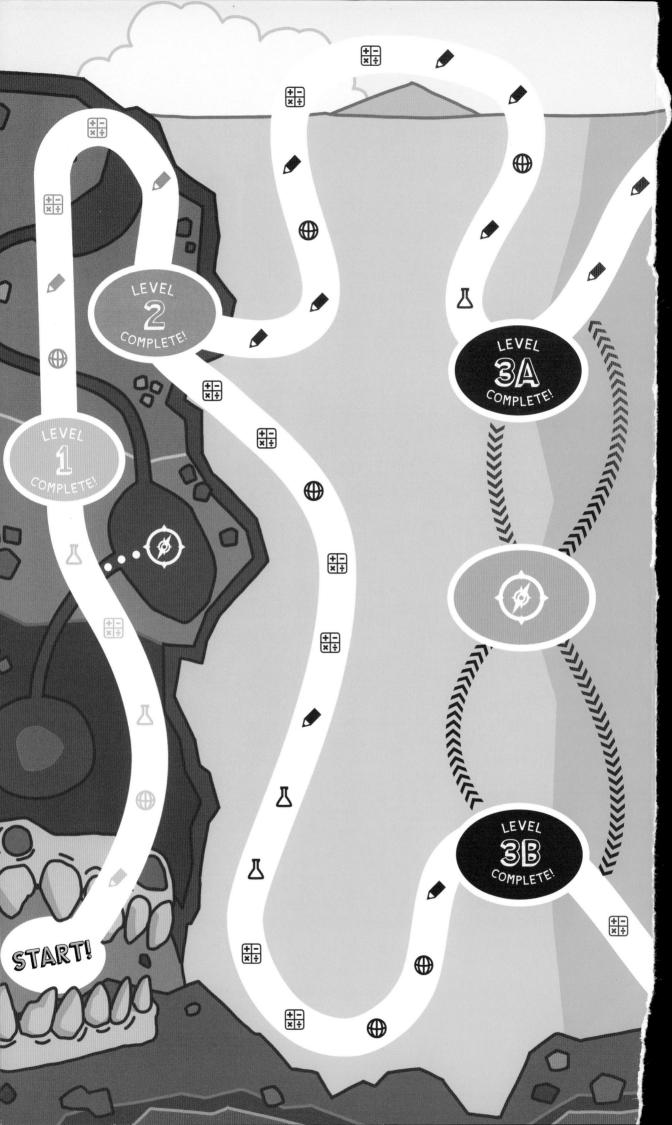

LEVEL 2 COMPLETE!

LEVEL 1 COMPLETE!

LEVEL 3A COMPLETE!

LEVEL 3B COMPLETE!

START!